portrait of a woman, impaled

Lilith.

for my father, whose radical faith in me saved
my life

and to all of the delusional bitches,
all of the end of the road people,
and all of the people brave enough
to hope and dream

THERE ARE NO STRAIGHT LINES

the light crawls across wet pavement
and i think of you.

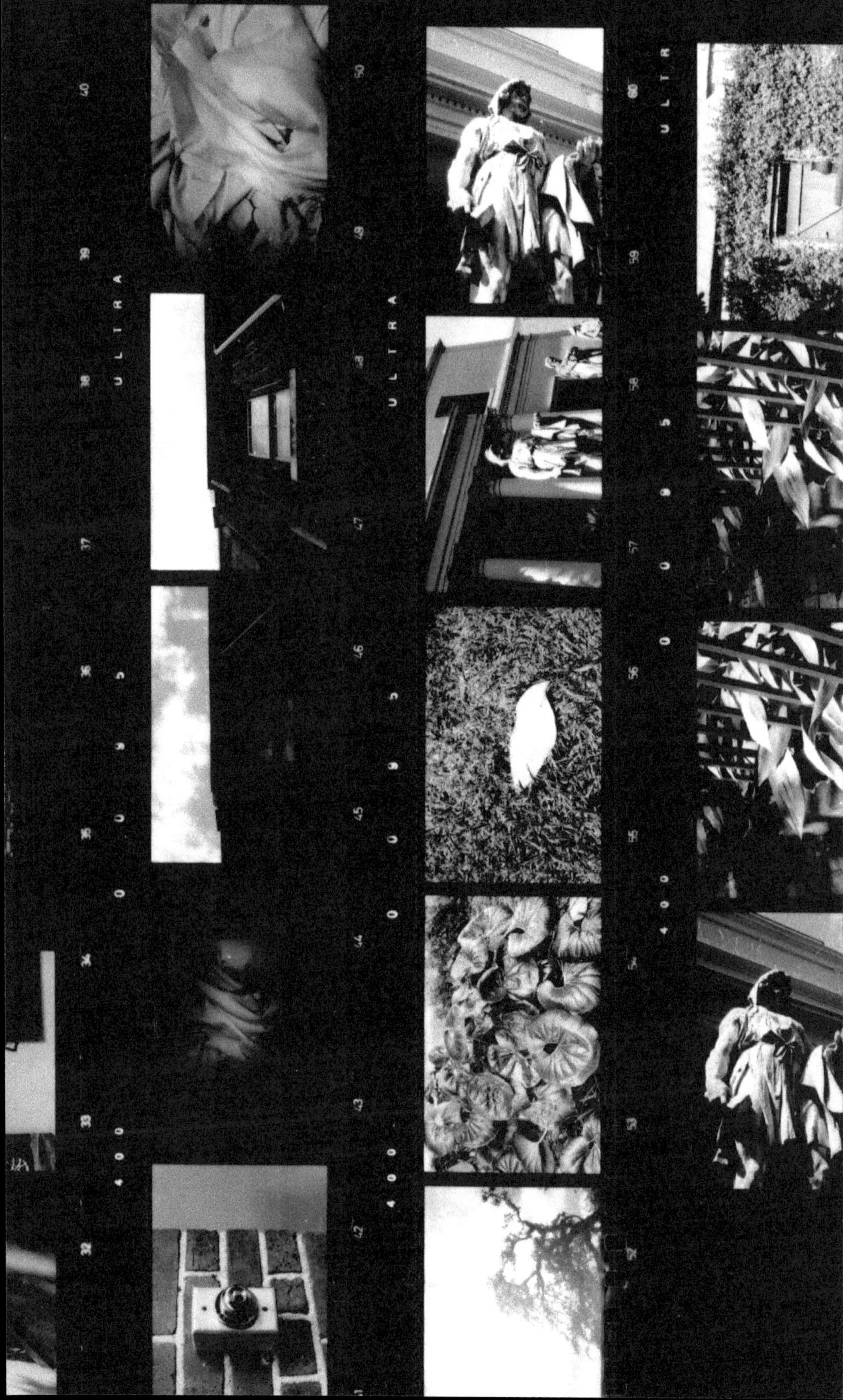

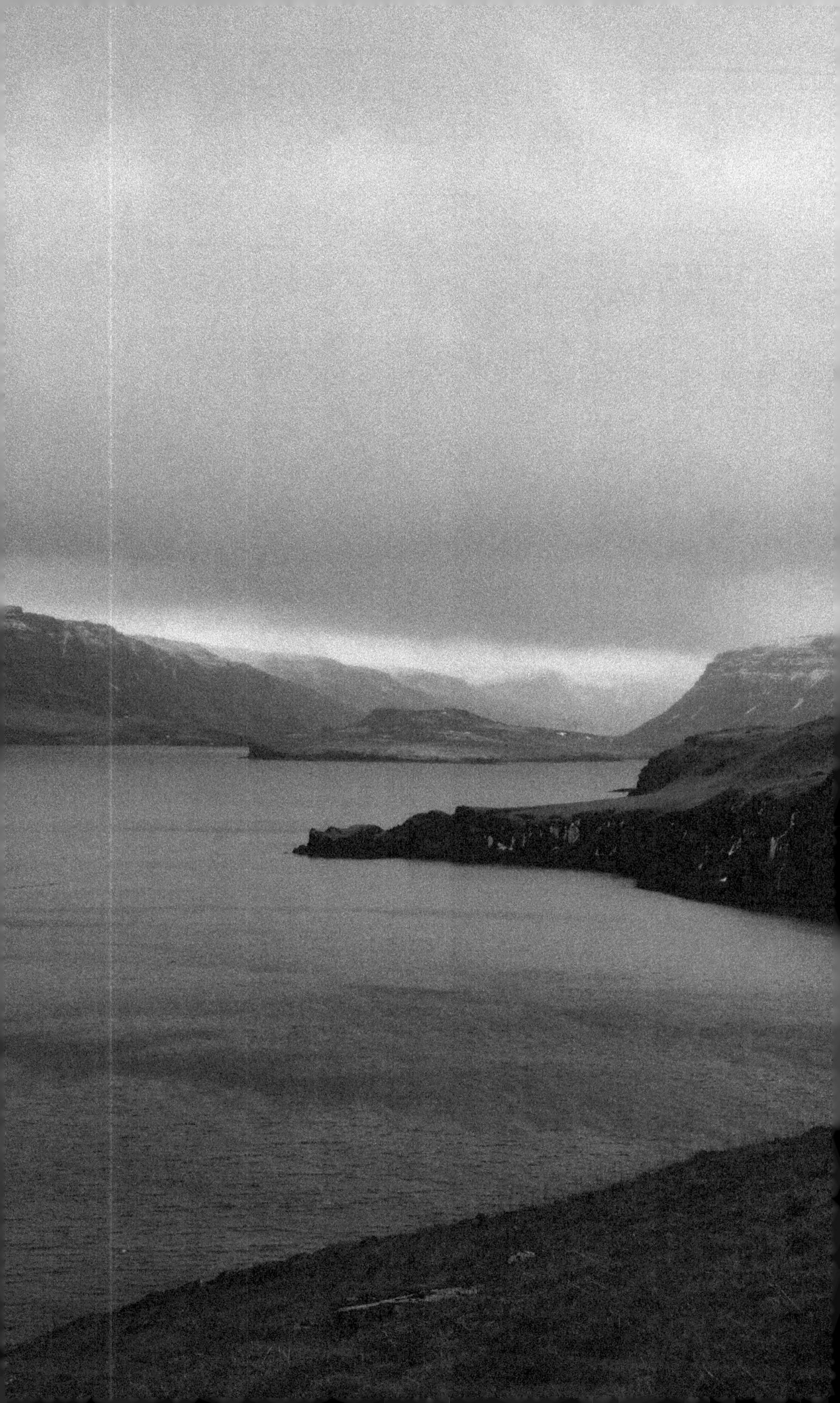

I

entry wound//entry wound//entry wound//entry wound

In the moment, it
stops making sense
and becomes
something new—
pressure cooked for
too long in the
memory of fourth of
July sweat above your
brow, June bugs, and
half-eaten
watermelon resting
on overgrown grass.

There is no good
explanation as to why
I held on this long.

Sometimes the truth
isn't told,
it's intrinsic.

there is a place where the dunes roll down right to the edge. they come to meet the water like a lover, and this is where i like to sit, tucked up between the washover channels and the sharp grass.

i come here at sunset, when i know i can be alone. today, the only other here is a gull, picking shells from the shallows, furiously searching for fresh meat.

i am raw today, exposed. there is no fortress around my heart— i am totally cracked open. it is a full moon, and the brutal waves curl like my upper lip when i'm trying not to cry. i am always holding back the tide. i feel the current trying to slip between the flesh of my ribs, but i am good. i am stronger now, i think, and so i make a promise— i will not tear again this time.

i notice the gull found himself a winner. looking closely, i believe his prize is called a lettered olive, impossible to get open with the beak alone; this is because the snail inside can curl backwards, retreat beyond reach into the narrow cavity behind the thick shell walls. he holds the problem between his beak for a moment, then in a beat, he takes off, flying upward. i watch as he goes higher, wondering where he is going. he flies over the dunes to the dry, windswept flat, and flapping in place against the wind, he drops the little cephalopod, house and all. the poor snail hurtles downward like a missile, point oriented perfectly towards the ground. there is no explosion with landfall. it's rather simple. the top of the shell pops off, and the rest breaks into several large pieces. the gull sweeps down, claiming it's now-shattered prize in one bite. i think — a lot of work for so little reward.

but now i am seeing myself. yes, this is how i break my own heart. i go so high, out of perspective, even when i try to curl away for safety, and then i drop myself. i fly down to inspect, and i mourn for the thing. then i eat the mess, becoming my own fuel. then after, i return to the shallows to pick around for fresh meat. this is how i break my own heart. it is nobody else's fault. i go on the hunt. i learned early on how to gamble. and i learned early on how to starve just a little bit. be happy with such small portions, working very hard for crumbs.

tucked up in the tall grass, i recognize myself for a moment. the beating tides. the lettered olive. the asshole bird, now looking at me with disdain in his little beady eyes. the dunes kissing the water. the washover fans. the grass-sheltered spot in the sand behind the dunes where certainly, at some point, two lovers have twisted and tied themselves together beneath a full moon like the one rising overhead. the salt in the cool wind.
the sun retreating behind the old pines.

i think to myself, there really is not much else to it. this is just how it is, how it will always be. the nature of it is survival. we all have to eat, no matter how little. some of us hunt big game, and some of us pick shells or carcasses and take what little we can find. inside and outside, the landscape is the same. the puzzle is not hard to put together, but you'll take too long if you're afraid of looking at the big picture that finds itself in the space between the pieces. and the thing is, time is running out. dunes are eroding, falling back every year. the lover's kiss is too strong, sweeping away the substance of the thing with hands too heavy and warm. today i see that things are changing, inside and out.

it is getting dark now, and the timer inside my ribs ticks a little faster as i brush the sand off my ass and turn towards the trail leading me back to my truck. i think i'll go home tomorrow.

3/23/23
1:32 am

dead bird

i've quietly
written the book
on you
(and regret)

i spent
8 years
with other people
and now i grieve

the possibility that
i won't be forgiven
for my hubris

i pray
and pray
and pray

that i am the prodigal daughter
but i think maybe

you are the sun.
and i am icarus

3/28/23
7:43 am

eternal flame

i watch
my earliest
most tender dreams
curl and shrink and smoke
in the flames
they convulse once or twice
and let out a death rattle
that almost breaks my heart
—almost
but they burn long
longer than they should
i'm still waiting
on the fizzle
final blow
rapture
and the end won't come
to release me into the realm of grief

why do you
burn forever
in such a meager way?
i am not warm enough to survive here
but i cannot leave knowing you could
one day set my world on fire
all over again
with just an ember.

4/07/23
12:58 pm

wimbledon

my aunt was
stillborn—
an object burnt up
upon re-entry into the atmosphere
ozone friction, too much for her

still borne into this
my grandmother still speaks fondly;
her first and last breath, the same
perhaps not the worst fate
knowing how things were in that home

a suffering bud, nipped
before blossom

but for those of us here
watching the wilting of the mother
there is a gap we all mind

i know there is no such
closureless pain
as what might've been
a whole life with a ghost
a phantom of could've

i feel much the same way about this.

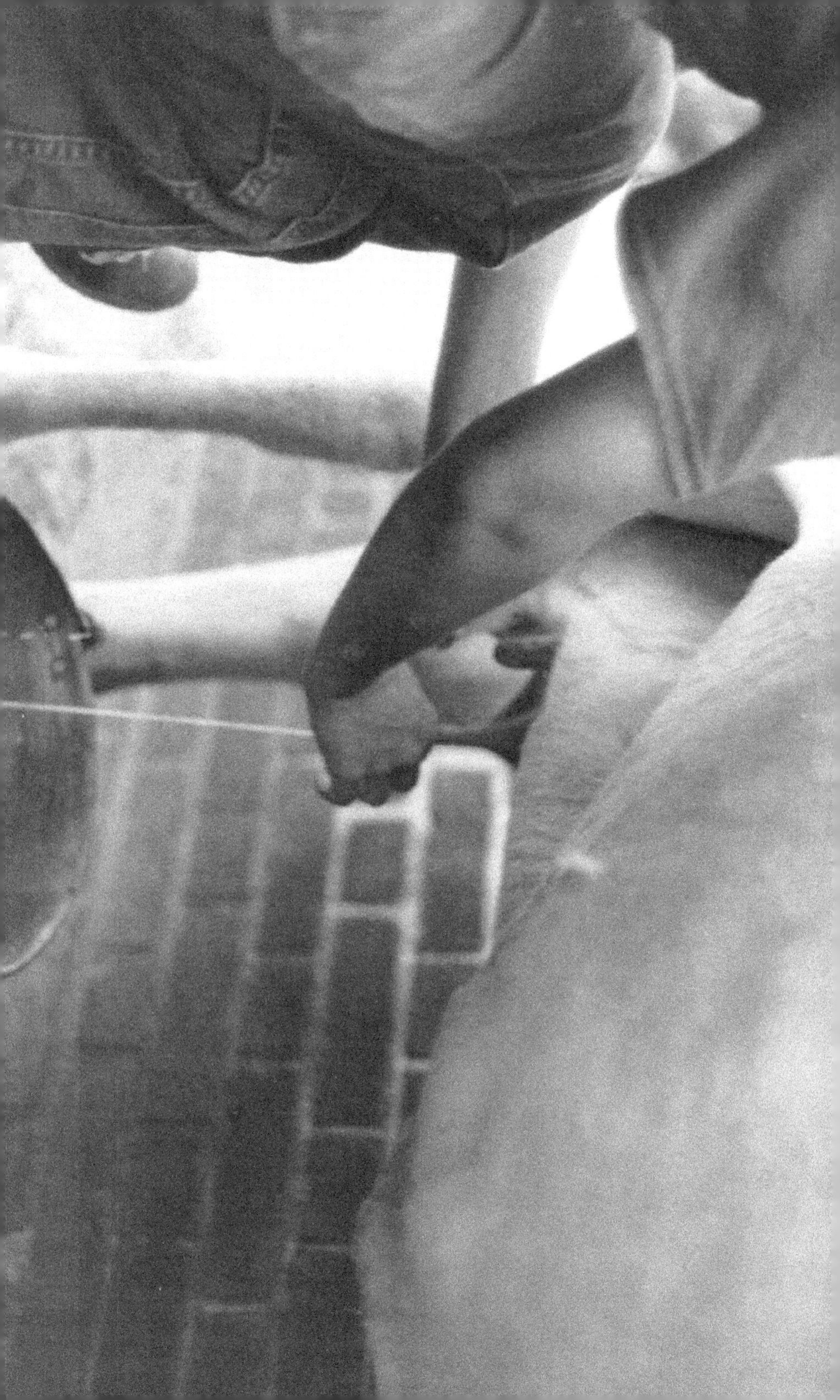

3/28/23
4:44 pm

in the winter of 2014
everything caught on fire
my sister's hands
my mother's nerves
my father's last chance at happiness
everything fell apart
turpentine filled my lungs
and bled the colors
until all that was left was grey

i scrambled to put the pieces back together
place all the marbles back in the tin
but i couldn't
i needed something
anything
so i started making choices
and they follow me even now
that every cell in my body has replaced itself
one and a half times over

i didn't realize
saviors don't exist
there is no magic man
just people who may
lay some bricks with you
or kick your sand castles
or pour gasoline all over your clothes
flick the match
and step back to watch you burn

anyone can choose to be a monster
usually it is on accident
i've dabbled in monstrosity myself
setting people on fire
because i needed to be warm somehow
i always stay too close
and everyone gets burnt

but the most cruel thing about me
is that every heart i've ever
ignited
i lit with a flame
i took from a heart
i never got to touch
a sick pilot light inside me
burning what-if's and i-wish-i-had's
that make me wonder—
if i ever even had a heart
of my own to give

like a baby switched at birth
it's chronic
and i haven't felt right
since the sky exploded on the 4th of july
before the crumbling
you were the last face i really saw
before i died that november

i know where home is
but i've never been
and i don't know if i'll ever get there

4/18/23
10:14 pm

once, we dreamed in tandem
before the possession
took my body
like a glove
to a cruel hand

before, legend has it
i burned down the cathedral
and turned over the orange CJ-7 on 95
before i blinked out
a cell tower flashed
behind the coal mountains
and i thought of you
in the passenger seat
as the fog rolled through
in 2021

3 years since we spoke
about the taliban and yellow velvet pants
and horrible things happened in the mean time

i missed you

the red thread stretched thin
and now that i came back
it may be too much to reel in
and i miss you
right here

where i was the last time
where i've always been

resurrection ferns
and the sunrise
some things come back
i am one of them

5/13/23
11:53 pm

my heart
will always be
warped in
your direction.

4/9/23
8:52 am

i keep my love for you
with all the other things i hide
under my tongue
like a pill
i can't swallow
but don't want to spit out

i can't get caught
and i think it might be the medicine

i need

3/2/23
9:50 am

i'm afraid
and not a handful of live rounds
nor my sharp pocket knives
and not even my red lips
can make me brave
for this one—

i'm afraid of a future
where somebody loves me
better than you

but i still love you best

a dirty, unopened package
sitting inside my chest
that i can't ever return to sender

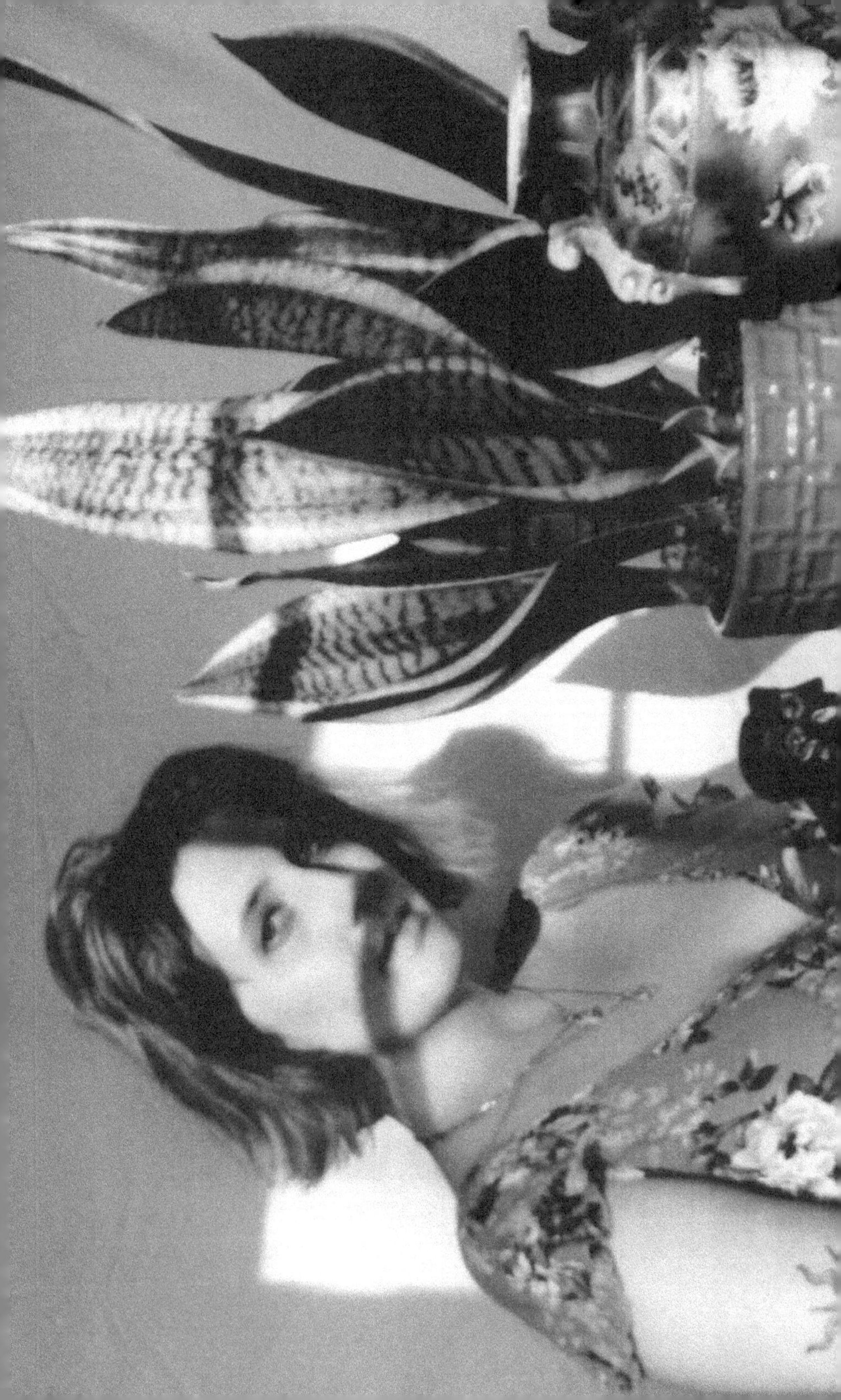

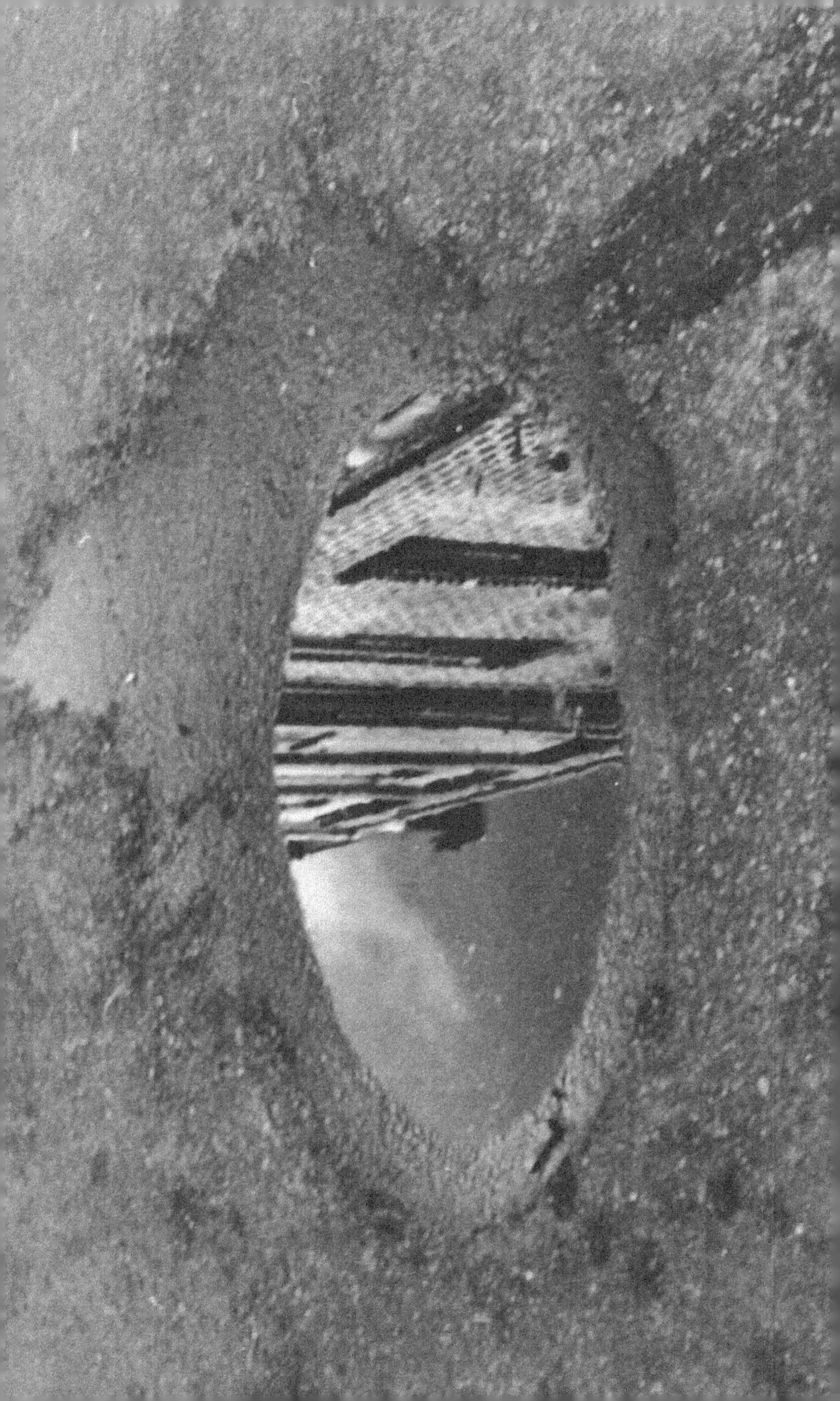

II

match sticks//match sticks//match sticks//matchsticks
match sticks//match sticks//match sticks//matchsticks
match sticks//match sticks//match sticks//matchsticks
match sticks//match sticks//match sticks//matchsticks
match sticks//match sticks//match sticks//matchsticks
match sticks//match sticks//match sticks//matchsticks
match sticks//match sticks//match sticks//matchsticks
match sticks//match sticks//match sticks//matchsticks
match sticks//match sticks//match sticks//matchsticks
match sticks//match sticks//match sticks//matchsticks
match sticks//match sticks//match sticks//matchsticks
match sticks//match sticks//match sticks//matchsticks
match sticks//match sticks//match sticks//matchsticks
match sticks//match sticks//match sticks//matchsticks
match sticks//match sticks//match sticks//matchsticks
match sticks//match sticks//match sticks//matchsticks
match sticks//match sticks//match sticks//matchsticks
match sticks//match sticks//match sticks//matchsticks
match sticks//match sticks//match sticks//matchsticks
match sticks//match sticks//match sticks//matchsticks
match sticks//match sticks//match sticks//matchsticks
match sticks//match sticks//match sticks//matchsticks
match sticks//match sticks//match sticks//matchsticks
match sticks//match sticks//match sticks//matchsticks
match sticks//match sticks//match sticks//matchsticks
match sticks//match sticks//match sticks//matchsticks
match sticks//match sticks//match sticks//matchsticks
match sticks//match sticks//match sticks//matchsticks
match sticks//match sticks//match sticks//matchsticks
match sticks//match sticks//match sticks//matchsticks
match sticks//match sticks//match sticks//matchsticks
match sticks//match sticks//match sticks//matchsticks
match sticks//match sticks//match sticks//matchsticks
match sticks//match sticks//match sticks//matchsticks
match sticks//match sticks//match sticks//matchsticks
match sticks//match sticks//match sticks//matchsticks
match sticks//match sticks//match sticks//matchsticks
match sticks//match sticks//match sticks//matchsticks
match sticks//match sticks//match sticks//matchsticks
match sticks//match sticks//match sticks//matchsticks
match sticks//match sticks//match sticks//matchsticks
match sticks//match sticks//match sticks//matchsticks
match sticks//match sticks//match sticks//matchsticks
match sticks//match sticks//match sticks//matchsticks
match sticks//match sticks//match sticks//matchsticks
match sticks//match sticks//match sticks//matchsticks
match sticks//match sticks//match sticks//matchsticks
match sticks//match sticks//match sticks//matchsticks
match sticks//match sticks//match sticks//matchsticks
match sticks//match sticks//match sticks//matchsticks
match sticks//match sticks//match sticks//matchsticks
match sticks//match sticks//match sticks//matchsticks
match sticks//match sticks//match sticks//matchsticks
match sticks//match sticks//match sticks//matchsticks
match sticks//match sticks//match sticks//matchsticks
match sticks//match sticks//match sticks//matchsticks
match sticks//match sticks//match sticks//matchsticks
match sticks//match sticks//match sticks//matchsticks
match sticks//match sticks//match sticks//matchsticks
match sticks//match sticks//match sticks//matchsticks
match sticks//match sticks//match sticks//matchsticks
match sticks//match sticks//match sticks//matchsticks
match sticks//match sticks//match sticks//matchsticks
match sticks//match sticks//match sticks//matchsticks
match sticks//match sticks//match sticks//matchsticks
match sticks//match sticks//match sticks//matchsticks

I'm going west—
so I can stand alone in the spaces
I wish I could share with you.

With the wind twisting my hair into
thickets and the chill painting rose
petals on my cheeks,
I'll feel the phantom of a hand I
never held.

Two matchsticks that burnt out the
instant they were struck,
like firing off a flare
in the middle of a flood.

I'm night-riding far away from here,
where I have remembered you
so many nights.
Maybe out there,
it won't hurt quite so bad.

4/18/23
2:17 am

i broke myself on the chain
skipping lines on vinyl
every time i tried to turn away
defying a forgotten god
it should've been you before
and now you're all there is for me

1/23/23
10:48 pm

hope is dangerous
it's a handover
at gunpoint
do i give you this
crucial piece of my desire
and do i trust that you will not drop it?
a newborn or a china cup
or a tiny crystal figurine of a swan
these are her

we were both children once
who, at least one time
didn't get what we needed
and you get used to it, you know?
you get used to believing
that everything spoils like fruit
you give up to a sour milk destiny
and the concept of
do your best
never being enough to be really happy

there is a pain calling out
trying to talk over the light
but the glow of the sun on your cheeks—
it still glimmers and spatters freckles
even when the water is hitting
the top of your head
and all you can hear is the thumping
of niagara against your own skull
and when the icy falls roar and chill you
the sun still hits your skin
when you're 10 feet underwater
at the bottom of a swimming pool
light doesn't hear noise
and it travels through air and water
and it tells you
light speaks
of the inevitable
the sun will come up
and i will, too

so please keep your eyes open for me.

?/??/??

a prophesy

a bird flies
at its own reflection
unaware of its
impending
collision

1/24/23
8:27 pm

what i would do to you

lick the salt from your wounds—
i want to see all the parts that hurt

kiss off the bruises left
by a careless brother
and suck out the venom
left in you the first time grief took a bite

i want to drink the blood
that fell from your wrist
the first time anger sliced you
with a serrated edge—
how unfair could things be?

i want to find the scrapes
and spread my own tears in you
like a salve
dripping spit

i want to bite down
on the skin
behind your neck
and carry you home

safe.

4/18/23
8:08 pm

i haven't slept right in years
i think i distract myself
from how exhausting it is
to be alert all the time
waiting for her to come through my door
demanding me
and i think maybe
my grief has a home at night
and i have to keep the light on
so it can find its way around

i think i'd sleep
if you were here
i'd sleep for a month, probably

waking up from the nightmare
my head would hit the pillow
softly this time
not heavy with liquor
and fire
and the dark matter
with a gravitational pull
stronger than the sun
that all the ones i invited in
left with me

i daydream
of sleeping next to you
of breathing deep and heavy
of not waking up hungover with
imprints of my nails on my palms
and the sheets wrapped around my neck
like a noose

i'm afraid to sleep now
i don't want to go back there
the only time i feel okay
is when i dream about you
but then i wake up
and you haven't arrived yet

come soon
i've been waiting forever
to close my eyes
without knowing for certain
it won't go well

1/21/23
8:47 pm

brutal face
you vanished
but i'm an addict
don't you know?
hooked on the rushing
the reeding
i wade through the marsh in my mind

i'm on to you
wherever you are
a flash of light
can't erase a tenner

every night i whisper my call
begging, do not let this be driftwood
praying for roots
where there may be
just an over-tilled field

grief holds me like a lover

22

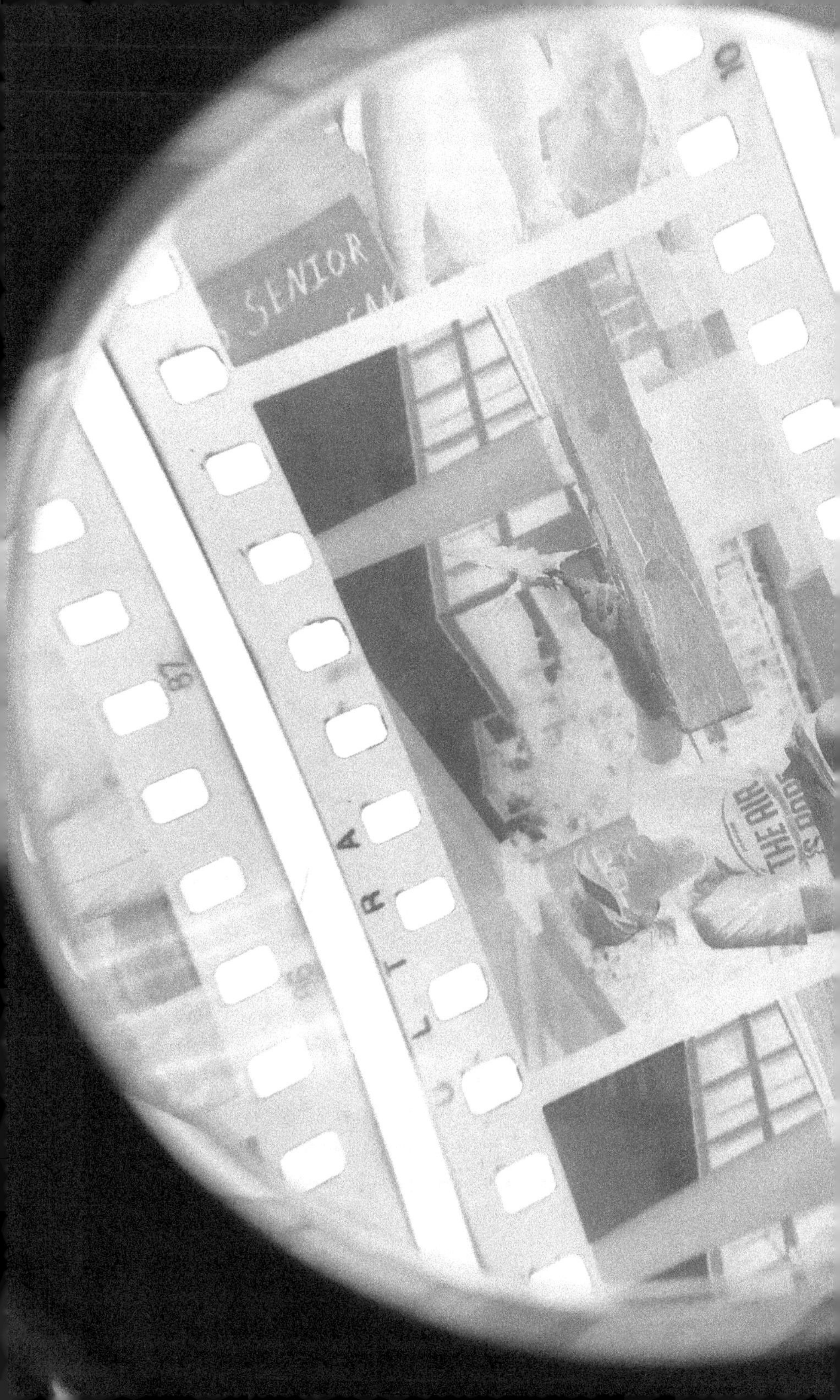
SENIOR
THE AIR

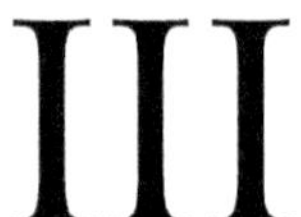

To be clear: this isn't about love.
No— this is about a path I never took.

Wishing for something impossible,
growing up bargaining with the things I struggle to accept;
(mainly, the what-ifs).

Trading dreams and fantasies for stones with which to fill my pockets.

swap meet//swap meet//swap meet//swap meet//swap meet
swap meet//swap meet//swap meet//swap meet//swap meet
swap meet//swap meet//swap meet//swap meet//swap meet
swap meet//swap meet//swap meet//swap meet//swap meet
swap meet//swap meet//swap meet//swap meet//swap meet
swap meet//swap meet//swap meet//swap meet//swap meet
swap meet//swap meet//swap meet//swap meet//swap meet
swap meet//swap meet//swap meet//swap meet//swap meet
swap meet//swap meet//swap meet//swap meet//swap meet
swap meet//swap meet//swap meet//swap meet//swap meet
swap meet//swap meet//swap meet//swap meet//swap meet
swap meet//swap meet//swap meet//swap meet//swap meet
swap meet//swap meet//swap meet//swap meet//swap meet
swap meet//swap meet//swap meet//swap meet//swap meet
swap meet//swap meet//swap meet//swap meet//swap meet
swap meet//swap meet//swap meet//swap meet//swap meet
swap meet//swap meet//swap meet//swap meet//swap meet
swap meet//swap meet//swap meet//swap meet//swap meet
swap meet//swap meet//swap meet//swap meet//swap meet
swap meet//swap meet//swap meet//swap meet//swap meet
swap meet//swap meet//swap meet//swap meet//swap meet
swap meet//swap meet//swap meet//swap meet//swap meet
swap meet//swap meet//swap meet//swap meet//swap meet
swap meet//swap meet//swap meet//swap meet//swap meet
swap meet//swap meet//swap meet//swap meet//swap meet
swap meet//swap meet//swap meet//swap meet//swap meet
swap meet//swap meet//swap meet//swap meet//swap meet
swap meet//swap meet//swap meet//swap meet//swap meet
swap meet//swap meet//swap meet//swap meet//swap meet
swap meet//swap meet//swap meet//swap meet//swap meet
swap meet//swap meet//swap meet//swap meet//swap meet
swap meet//swap meet//swap meet//swap meet//swap meet
swap meet//swap meet//swap meet//swap meet//swap meet
swap meet//swap meet//swap meet//swap meet//swap meet
swap meet//swap meet//swap meet//swap meet//swap meet
swap meet//swap meet//swap meet//swap meet//swap meet
swap meet//swap meet//swap meet//swap meet//swap meet
swap meet//swap meet//swap meet//swap meet//swap meet
swap meet//swap meet//swap meet//swap meet//swap meet
swap meet//swap meet//swap meet//swap meet//swap meet
swap meet//swap meet//swap meet//swap meet//swap meet
swap meet//swap meet//swap meet//swap meet//swap meet
swap meet//swap meet//swap meet//swap meet//swap meet
swap meet//swap meet//swap meet//swap meet//swap meet
swap meet//swap meet//swap meet//swap meet//swap meet
swap meet//swap meet//swap meet//swap meet//swap meet
swap meet//swap meet//swap meet//swap meet//swap meet
swap meet//swap meet//swap meet//swap meet//swap meet
swap meet//swap meet//swap meet//swap meet//swap meet
swap meet//swap meet//swap meet//swap meet//swap meet
swap meet//swap meet//swap meet//swap meet//swap meet
swap meet//swap meet//swap meet//swap meet//swap meet
swap meet//swap meet//swap meet//swap meet//swap meet
swap meet//swap meet//swap meet//swap meet//swap meet

1/27/23
6:36 pm

a conversation with a ghost

i will not be reduced
as most women are
to top and bottom

not that you ever
tried to pick my brain
and i always gave you more than you wanted

but i cannot see
why i am so misunderstood
i have always— always
(here is a sentence i am too afraid to finish)

however, i am not a simple person
as you may assume me to be
and i made a series of complicated decisions

betrayal— to you.

not asking me to
overlook context
not playing in the fucking sandbox.

the one thing i resent (speaking openly)
is that assumption of simplicity

maybe i complicated things too much
with my christ complex and verbal indigestion
maybe i have once again

held too loosely
to the right thing.
(it's never really over)

3/2/23
1:29 pm

why do you
clip the wings
of the angel trying to save you?

if you'd let me,
i'd show you something worth living for.

but your engine's misfiring
and you won't hop in with me
so i sit here
beating my typewriter

holding out for Perseus, not yet ready
to leave aeaea
for the real world—

bright and briny
and there are flowers for you here
and there are flowers for you here.

let me bring them to you.

10/9/22
9:03 pm

breathing in the
sunlight filtering through the leaves
i counted the stars
and made constellations
out of your paint splatter skin

i didn't know i'd remember this
i didn't know i'd remember then

i wish i could
roll a decade up
like a persian rug

and trip and fall right back there
just to feel it again

i would bring a jar
to catch the air between us
and collect the cicada shells
we stepped over
underneath the laurel

maybe we too
would be poison
if we allowed ourselves to burn

2/16/23
1:41am

whatever you think is wrong with you,
i don't believe in it.

4/17/23
12:45 am

your love was confederate money to me
i was born empty on the railroad tracks at 23
and i didn't know where i was

i didn't know where i was
but i knew you were never real

i exchanged all my innocence for wisdom
and all my hope for regret
and the only man i ever loved
for a boat with a hole in the hull

i knew it was a mistake from the start

i didn't have a paddle and i was going down
i spent years searching for the sound
of another man's heart in his chest

but you and i, we know best
that's not how it works when it's real
that's not how it works out
that's not how

it was never real.

a prosthetic love
the hand is there
but it can't feel

a replacement for something
cut away long ago

every night
i bruise my knees
praying that it'll grow back
and i'll feel myself touch someone new

maybe there is no god
but i ask anyway

i left a part of me out there somewhere
i ran
i walked
now i crawl
back

i hope it'll still be where i left it.

2/9/23
11:09 pm

i've gotten so comfortable
with the idea that i might be
forever trapped inside my mind

you scare me
because what if
what am i going to do
if i let myself think i'm wrong

and you prove me right again?

turning keys
breathing lies that turn out to be the truth,
feeling you against me
what if i do all of this
settling in

and i'm still right?

what if you see all of me

and it's the last piece i show you
that makes you decide

that you don't want me as i am?

4/21/23
1:45 pm

i am not to you
what you are to me
which

in reality
is what she is for you
i know your pain—

why you can't love me
is the same reason
i can't love him

we're both looking back
holding the door open
for someone unlikely
to follow us through

but i think maybe
i deserve to have
the door held for me

just this once

2/28/23
11:25 pm

i'm halfway to 24
and i still associate
you with cadmium red
and a hand on my wrist
pulled me off to Boston
but i still
call you a home i've never had
and god it hurts
like a black eye
i can see in the mirror
but nobody else knows
this hole in my chest
is the shaped like your palm
and my eyes are bloodshot
because i can't fill it

3/13/23
2:07 am

dolphins in the winter
do you like it here?
would
you?
the fine line between desperation
and excitement
you have some of who i fell in love with first
and a lot of redactions

so much i want to tell you
so much i want to know
do you feel the chill all the way to the spine?
does it punch you in the chest?
hurting like a hammer to the four knuckles
of your left hand?
does it make your teeth rattle around like
marbles in a ball jar?
or is there some part of me
that could keep you warm?
do i keep you warm?

no, i'm not really talking about the snow.

5/24/23
12:07pm

swap meet

they go
they go
they go

but some people remain

you take a part
and give a part

and though you are
apart

they remain

inside of you

where they once were

in the literal sense

they now

live

immortalized

etched deeply

into the walls of your heart

graffiti left behind by
loving vandals

unalterable

immovable

in a place that does not follow rules

of time

or distance

and certainly

does not know death

or endings of any sort

some things are forever.

IV

If things had been different —

2/7/23
7:26am
i am done with thankless jobs
no longer sisyphus

?/?/??
my wings
feel heavy.

6/6/23
2:09 pm

there is a thing living in my chest
with soft hair
and a quivering lip
eyes as big as the moon
filling with mist
whenever someone comes too near

her hands tremble
and her breath catches
in her throat
because she is so small

like a child
but this beast is ancient
and drenched in fear
she dreams of those
who laid cruel hands on her
and shredded the garment she was born in

she stays naked now
in the cold
waiting and recoiling
hope and terror
in tempo with the beat of my heart

i protect her
by keeping her hidden
but you'll catch a glimpse
if you stay still long enough

approach slowly;
she knows there's nowhere left to run.

7/5/23
6:22 pm

i wonder how magical
all of this would've felt
if i hadn't been so fucking terrified

like living the whole thing
with my head shrouded in cling wrap

hands shaking in intervals
body relaxing just enough
to receive it all
but not quite enjoy
the middle bits fully

i loved him being there
but falling in love with him
tore my hands from the wheel
and made me sick

like hanging off a cliff
losing grip one finger at a time

i think any reasonable person
doubts that the person waiting below
will catch them

and i'm being reasonable this time

1/26/23
12:55 pm

i've tried killing it
a million different ways

slash and burn
getting under
running very very far
finding colder air to exhale
my cigarette smokestacks into

but i look for you

chasing dark eyes
down alleyways
and up the country
but they're unfamiliar—
not you.

something about this is unfair
for everyone involved

so, i'm passing out apologies all around:

i don't know if it's not dead yet
because it's unkillable
or if i just can't bring myself
to press the barrel between
dark eyes
and pull the trigger

5/24/23
1:01 pm

let's find a reason
a mutual truth
to break ourselves

on a blade
sharp enough
to split us in half—
separate parts, again

it's stretched thin
between two points
on a map of the world
scissors dull, thread intact

you unraveled me
you took more than i meant to give
but it was my fault too
for tying a knot
for every break

4/20/23
12:39 pm

i wanted to tell you
all the difficult parts
i wanted to whisper them
between kisses

why it was hard to leave
what i always believed in
when i thought i could come back and get it
once i was done
being busy
beating myself to death
on an idiot's fists
to prove a point to me

i thought i could come back
when i was ready
and i was ready

when i found out there was nothing
to come back to
nothing left to get
nothing left to believe in

forever truth
a figment god
alive in my mind
dead in the streets

a failure in lover's praxis

so why do i still feel you
in my chest?
did i make the magic the whole time
collecting dust with a glass of wine in the bathtub
knitting for myself with the wild yarn i spun
all on my own?

i'd still go so far
if we'd smile at each other
just one more time

but i won't turn to look
and you won't tap my shoulder
we can't stand here forever
it's going to rain soon
if you ever pick up a copy
you'll notice the ink was running the whole time

but i wrote these words inside
i wrote these words inside

my garden dried up in your drought
why would i go out for dead daises?
the bluebirds don't even come around anymore.

2/20/23
6:43am

underneath i am curling
convulsing
kicking like a fetus in the womb
something brewing
simple evil solemn
death in a new way

i deliver myself once again
a paper boat floating over the edge
niagara is a killer.

3/25/23
1:47 am

reaching through the blackness
for something to cling to
like an anchor—

but i never knew how to sink
and he always knew how
to lay his weight on me
like steel.

3/29/23
12:19 am

i am not a checklist for you
and i never will be
walk away
before you're disappointed.

3/29/23
2:13am

i'm scared i might carve your name so deeply
into the doorframe of me
that nobody could ever love me but you
and you might choose

not to.

3/29/23
2:55pm

if i'm not already what you need
i cannot become it

4/1/23
12:52 am

the pierced tights darling
returns home
to rot in her room
to feel everything
in a place too sterile
i wake up every morning
with arms numb
and heart swollen

4/18/23
3:00 am

i've slept on the same side of this bed
for years
there's a divot now
where i've laid
and some people can sleep there
in the divot
they love it
the deeper it gets
the more hollow the space is
where they belong
they know they existed there
and so it is safe
in that 9 year old mattress
and not just any mattress
the mattress that held them for so long
and sometimes they go on vacation
and they miss the divot
they can't sleep without it

right now
i am lying awake in my hole

and i think what i'm trying to say is that
it couldn't be just anyone

5/5/23
2:25 am

shadow boxing with the memories
that seep out of the cracks in my skull

pulled over by the cemetery
had to go somewhere that feels right

every night
i sneak back to you
alone in my bed

i come home.

i wish it was real
i wish it worked

lying to all the men
who loved me

lying to myself

because i have no god
but i believe in you

faithful
against my will

papers with just your name
scrawled across ten thousand times

a different religion
maybe in another life,
we are.

got to be.

i wish i could see it.

5/13/23
4:18 pm

my lust
is brining
in the ice box
a dish i make for you
but serve to those
whose opinion of my cooking
i don't care to ask

i'll always save you a seat at the table

5/17/23
3:09 pm

i had a nightmare

you and i
were together
on the couch
holding hands
watching something
david attenborough

and you looked at me
and you brushed the hair out of my eyes
and you said "i love you,"

sunlight filled my chest
i have never felt so happy
in my life

and then there was this beating
in my right ear
it came through
into the dream, slowly

thump thump
thump thump
thump thump

and i opened my eyes
to see a vista
the landscape of hair
sprawling across another man's chest

and it was a nightmare.

2/2/23
12:35 pm

i was taught to die
to quietly scream
to pour whiskey on it

i was taught to swallow knives
to learn to see in the dark
to coil myself tightly

i was taught to donate all my thread
to leave holes in my shirts
to stick my hands in the boiling water

i was taught to be alone
to find the largest crowd and lose myself there
to shatter in silence

i was taught to stand uncovered in the rain
to gnash my teeth
to bother nobody with it all

there's no happy ending here
just more to learn
other things to look at

that has to be enough.

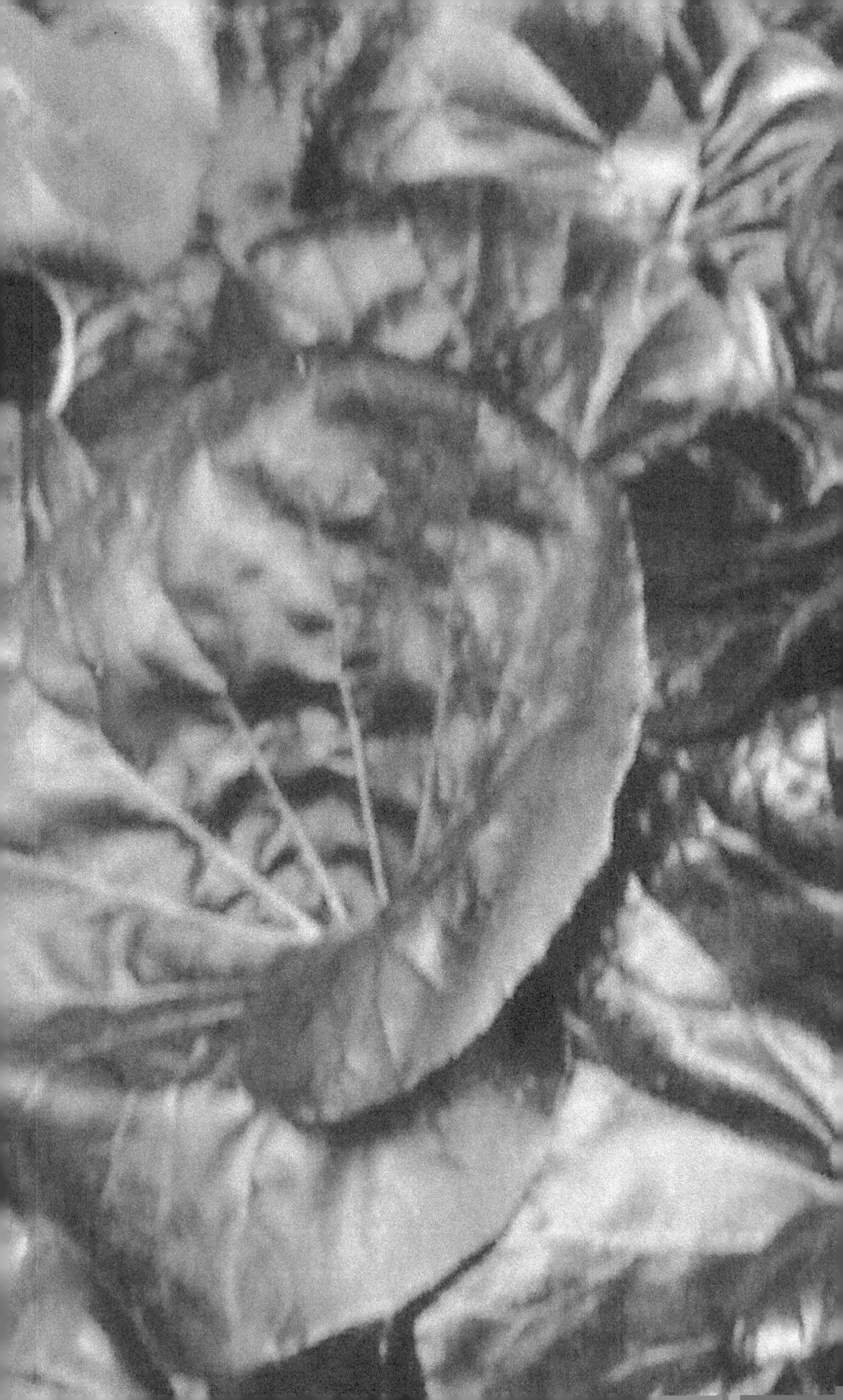

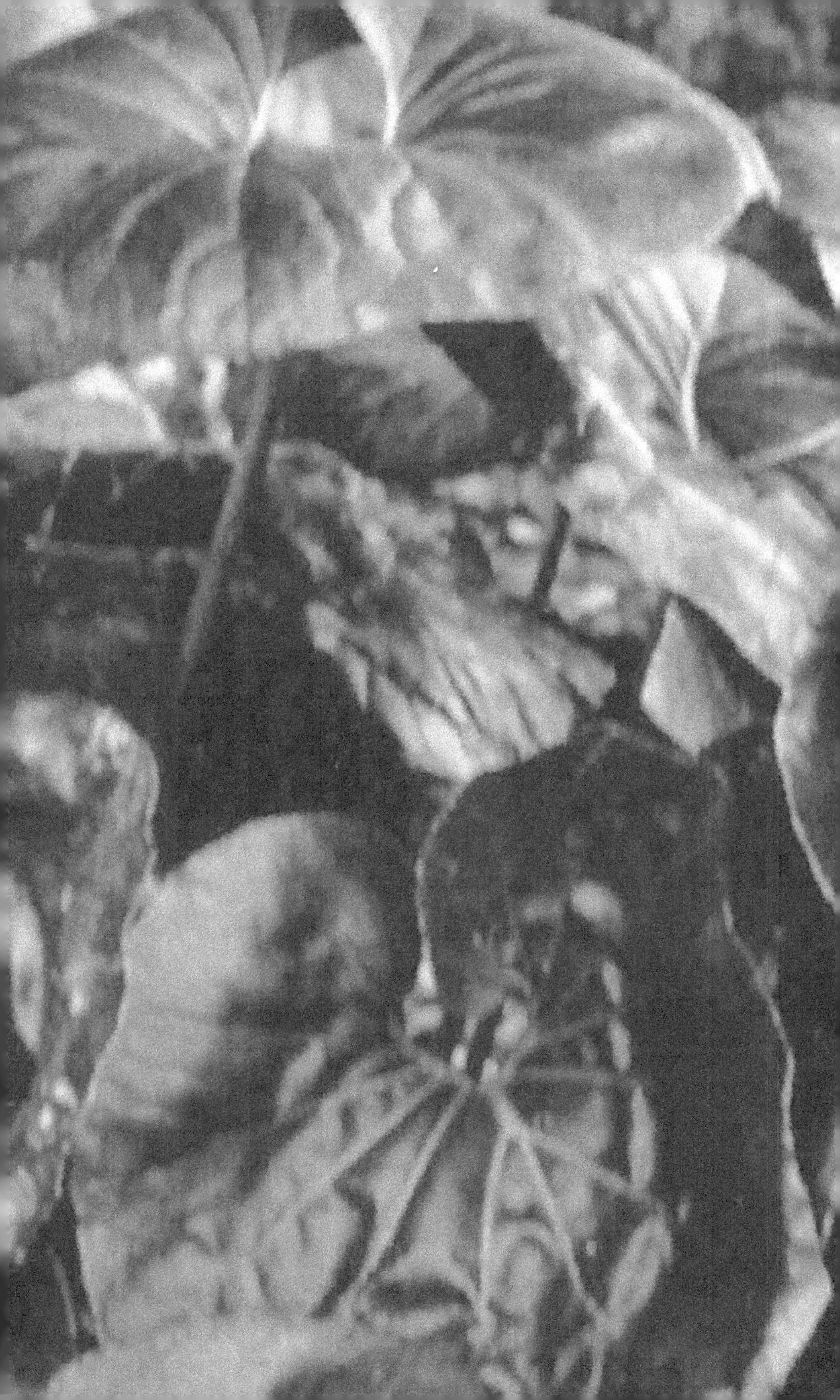

V

I have hubris — nothing is
lost to me, because I paint in
my own blood.

It's true, in the sense that I
am a fucking artist, and I can
make sense of scraps.
I make sense of you, my
shredded hopes; in tatters
about you.

Awake night after night —
none of those feelings were
wasted.

The colors I bled will go on a
clean canvas.
One day, I will reconcile
myself in somebody else's
heart.

That will mean more.

3/23/23
1:25am

i tried for so long to fit a million people into the print your body left in the grass next to me.

i tried to make people closer to me make sense. i tried to dress them up in you, but they were never you. i write good words—charming words. i wrote beautiful words for them.

but i wasn't writing about them. i was putting down all the dreams i had about you—and writing their name at the top. the miles between us hurt so much. and i needed some kind of drug to make it stop.

but anesthesia never lasts, and if you take too much, it'll kill you.

?/?/??

every quality
that i loved in you
i will find in someone else
no human exists
in a vacuum
i will love you
through their hearts

4/28/23
8:26 am

there is a moment of impact—
realizing that in spite of love
damage has occurred
that cannot be undone

no matter how much
i adore you

i can never trust you again
not in the same way

because i know now
what you're capable of.

even if we embrace,
my arms around your neck
would be albatross wings
your weight upon my chest
would make a sisyphus of me

always pushing away the truth
of how you treated my heart

when i offered it,
open and warm
on a golden platter
for the taking—

you took out a steak knife.

3/28/23
9:58 pm

i can catch a wave
i can learn from this
men tired and hungry
taught me my body is not
disgusting
but they also said
it was a form of sustenance
they wanted to live from me
and i was not a mother
could never be what they wanted
freudian and warm
i intellectualized all their
immaturity
studied them
stuck around for the science of it
took notes
but they took myself from me
and i gave myself to a god
unreal and burdened by expectation
of salvation
when even he cannot save on command
it is a bait and switch
you must decide yourself
if you are worth saving

i am worth saving,
i decided.
i am worth saving, by me and me alone.

3/30/23
8:58 pm

i want to take pictures of your face on film
show you my favorite spots
to hide from the world
my favorite loops to drive in
plan hypotheticals for the impending civil war
connect the dots on your cheeks
hold your head in the crook of my neck
feel your forehead against mine
paint you in a million colors
drive to see you
and drive home
and drive back again

you can't decide if you want me or not
and maybe you're right— or not ready
something in the way the wind sways the pines
makes me feel like you may be coming
picking your way slowly through the brush
waiting to see if i'll notice
just like in my dreams
but then again
the wind is cold
from the north
two doves land on the roof
of my father's home
and take off against the jetstream
i lay down in the grass to let the sun warm me
maybe this is all there is
purgatory breaths
the aching in my chest
ink smeared right hand
waiting for rapture
living like calypso
watching other men come and go
begging me to go with them
and saying No.
if i open the door to them
i close your door
and i won't do that again

i keep one eye on you
while i climb
towards the stronger me
no need for you to come with me on this one
but i don't want to leave you behind
so i'll always leave a light on
you know the key is under the mat

3/29/23
7:41 pm (abridged)

i wasn't a person until this year
i wasn't human
i was a hologram
programmed to serve
please
be quiet

i didn't have desires of my own
but to be good
a gym sock woman
an empty cup
an urn for other people's burnt wantings

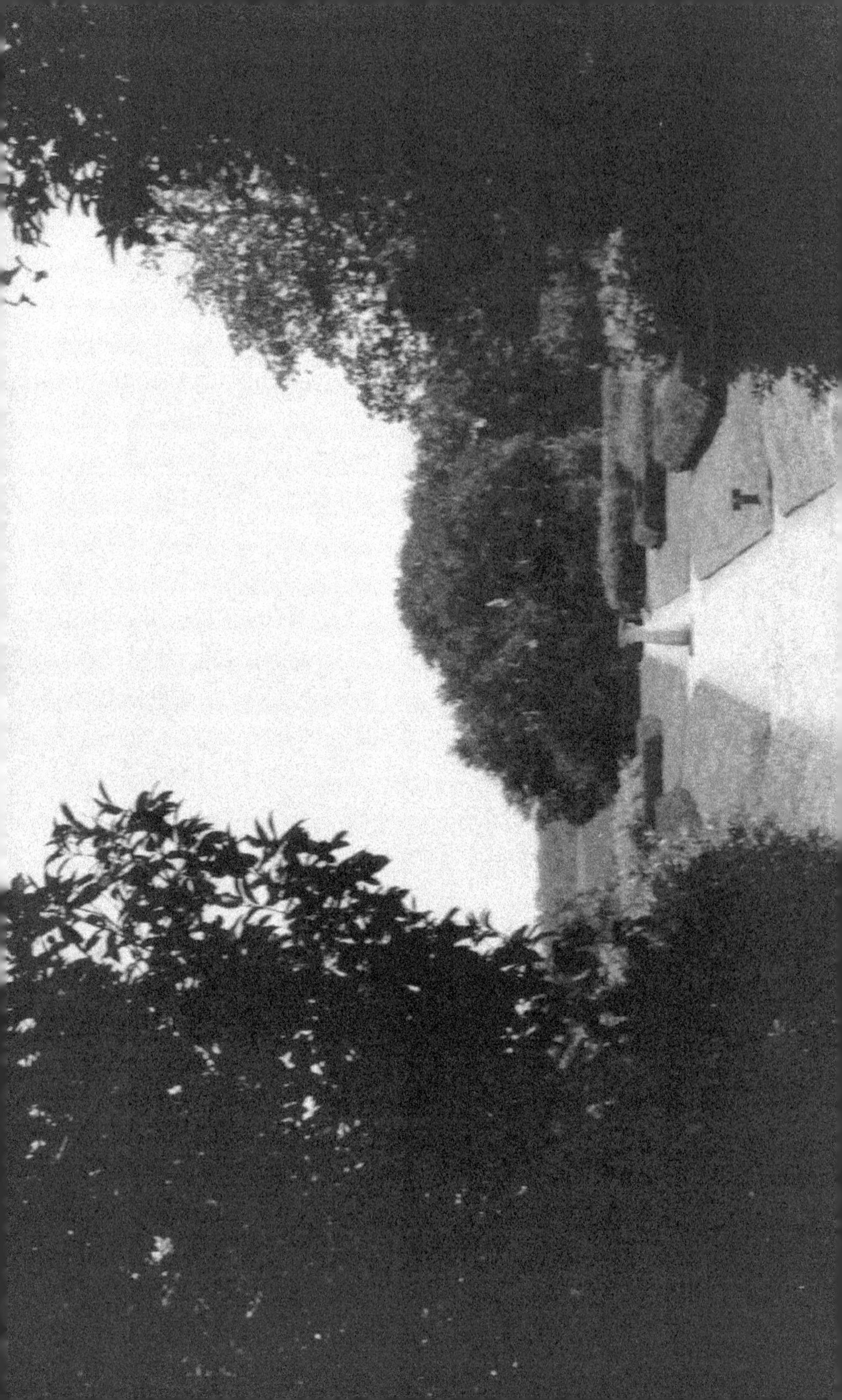

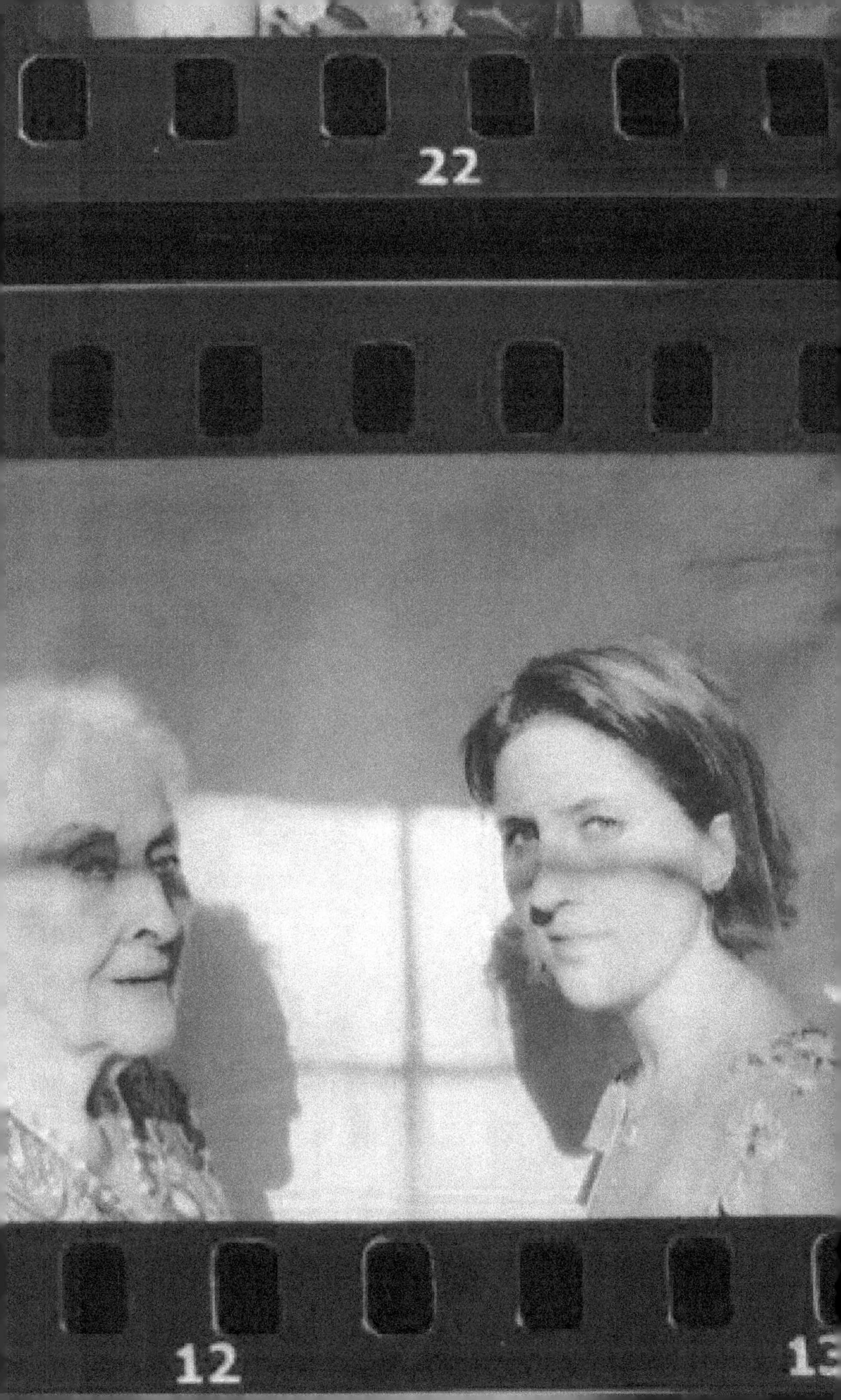
22
12
13

VI

Here's the thing that I think I forgot: the best, most powerful love is not based on some irrational attraction. It is built, brick by brick, slowly, and with intention. That moment of instant attraction is a flashbulb,

but good love is like the sun.

Adoration based in lust is not enough. Construction is necessary. Constant upkeep. How can I better understand you? How can I assist your happiness? How can I serve you? These things matter. Without these questions, we have nothing. All ether and no substance; we cannot survive on that.

2/19/23
2:24 am

and i feel myself
sliding bricks into place
walling up
something so fragile
so raw
open wounds blister in the sun
and i hold my own hand
again

12/27/22
2:07 am

i went out
and did all the things
i said i'd never do
and i discovered i was right
in the first place
about most things
it's kind of nice
knowing why
i said i'd never do them
now that i've finished
i can't uncrumple
i can't iron the creases
out of my mind
i can't unpierce
or unfuck
and i miss you
i miss who i left behind
but i'm glad for the lesson
the cement has been poured

1/4/23
8:47 pm

i fed my heart to the dogs
quick and messy
lapping up the blood; they said thank you
and saw themselves out

maybe i gave up
a styrofoam cup and a locket
she deserved more than a quarter; billions
and she got only a handshake

strange to know i'm breaking her
bite sized and empty
once i was small; now i am birdshot
and all i hold is this picnic basket
filled with rotten fruit

renovating after the fire
torn up blueprints and salvaged lumber
the guest bedroom is burning; one of us lived
and i am walking through after the gut

no longer playing pretend
hollow points and pocket knives
how i was razed; in the burn unit breathing ash
and this house will be more beautiful
than before the comet hit sand

it looks like i am playing in the cooling glass
but i am just picking pieces for the mosaic
hand to god; i will make something of this.

2/7/23
2:46 pm

i cheeked every pill that was given
to make me more digestible.

madness is a road
you must walk alone.

you cannot be mad
with someone;
it destroys the nature of the thing.

madness must be trodden
words later read by those literate
to this language…

in the moment of it,
you stand on an untouchable edge,
taking out the trash—
a one man job,
going deeper,
seeing farther than eyes can,
touching the bottom.

all this means less with a lifeline.

it can't make sense,
but the footprints of those mad for a moment
lead others out to the edge

10/11/22
2:52 am

one thing i'm not afraid of
is getting my heart broken
i've lived in it half my life
don't give me
something like cotton balls
and bandages
speak to me
honestly.

4/26/23
8:18 pm

a little girl died
opening up her eyes
man,
i can't do it anymore.
suffering for less
than minimum wage
none of your blood
follows me
flows to me
anymore.

i woke up a woman.
i woke up a woman
who knew
she loves you
but she shouldn't anymore.
anymore.

3/23/23
4:47 pm

i have never known bubble wrap
and i have never known a gentle hand
do we have any fucking sweets in this house?
my father cannot carry me any longer
bad back
broken feet
there is no cane to lean upon
no wand to cast the spell i need

i woke up from a dream where i birthed a baby i did not want
and i gave him to my dead friend
she held him gingerly in a way i could never
and i woke up and wrote the first part of my father's
eulogy
although he is not dead yet
i think i should tell him what i will say before he goes
through the swinging double doors

every day i disrespect the standard he set for me
i dropped the compass years ago
glass shattered
they do not make them like him anymore

and i am ready to be held like he held the wounded baby bird
i found in the glue trap
before we realized what he had to do
because her wings were too broken to fly again

is it me?

i want to be seen as deserving
instead of sucking on rusty nails and
eating hard boiled everything
but every needle
impaled me when i needed to be stitched up instead

i am emaciated and confused by the
way i dispense such gentle touch
never seen for how broken i am
i sweep your hair back softly because my bones
are weak
on the mend from greater crushes and strikes
than what you throw me from time to time

but the problem is
i ask for it
i do not know how not to
recoil from a hand un-firm
too kind
and i am afraid of what happens when the night turns
driving away my lily of the valley
manelich is me
pushing through the coolness of marta
but the sheep are all dead
there is nothing for me to go back to
a sham marriage is my nightmare too

so

i am here
scalp sore
hips hurting
wondering what it might feel like to be kissed first
asking how long it'll be before i know
before i let myself be known

asking
because i don't want to look at this much longer,
anybody got a fucking zoloft for me to chew on instead
of bankruptcy paperwork and hornets nests?

3/29/23
6:28 pm

i'm not agreeable
i'm not amenable
i'm unmatchable
not unlovable
but too much of myself
to become something for someone else
its either my perfect match
or nothing

4/23/23
11:19 pm

we might've been perfect
but you passed me up
when i turned back
and so now
i have to do
what i need to do.
i have to go.
you cannot become
my everything
when i am only a sliver to you.

i'm done.
i'm out.
i'm finished with this.
i wrote your name
a million times
just to come around
and say
honey
beloved
my long lost One
it was fun while it lasted.

but i am worth more
than second choice.

i am more
than this.

4/7/23
10:00 am

i feel alone most
when i'm surrounded
seeing everyone
dozing
while i am keeping watch

if any of them
could see inside
sit inside my mind
who among them would want
to stick around?

so much i never say
bleeding onto the page
all night long, just to
release some of the pressure. burning
who would understand?
want to understand?

maybe we all feel lonely this way
an open secret we all keep
just there, never spoken aloud,
that we are all trapped in our bodies
yearning for something more than touch
all candles staring at the sun,

wishing to be a part of it.

?/??/??

the endings we choose are perfect

so, goodbye perfect storm, favorite illusion
i need no fantasy in the present

so i think i'll stay here awhile.

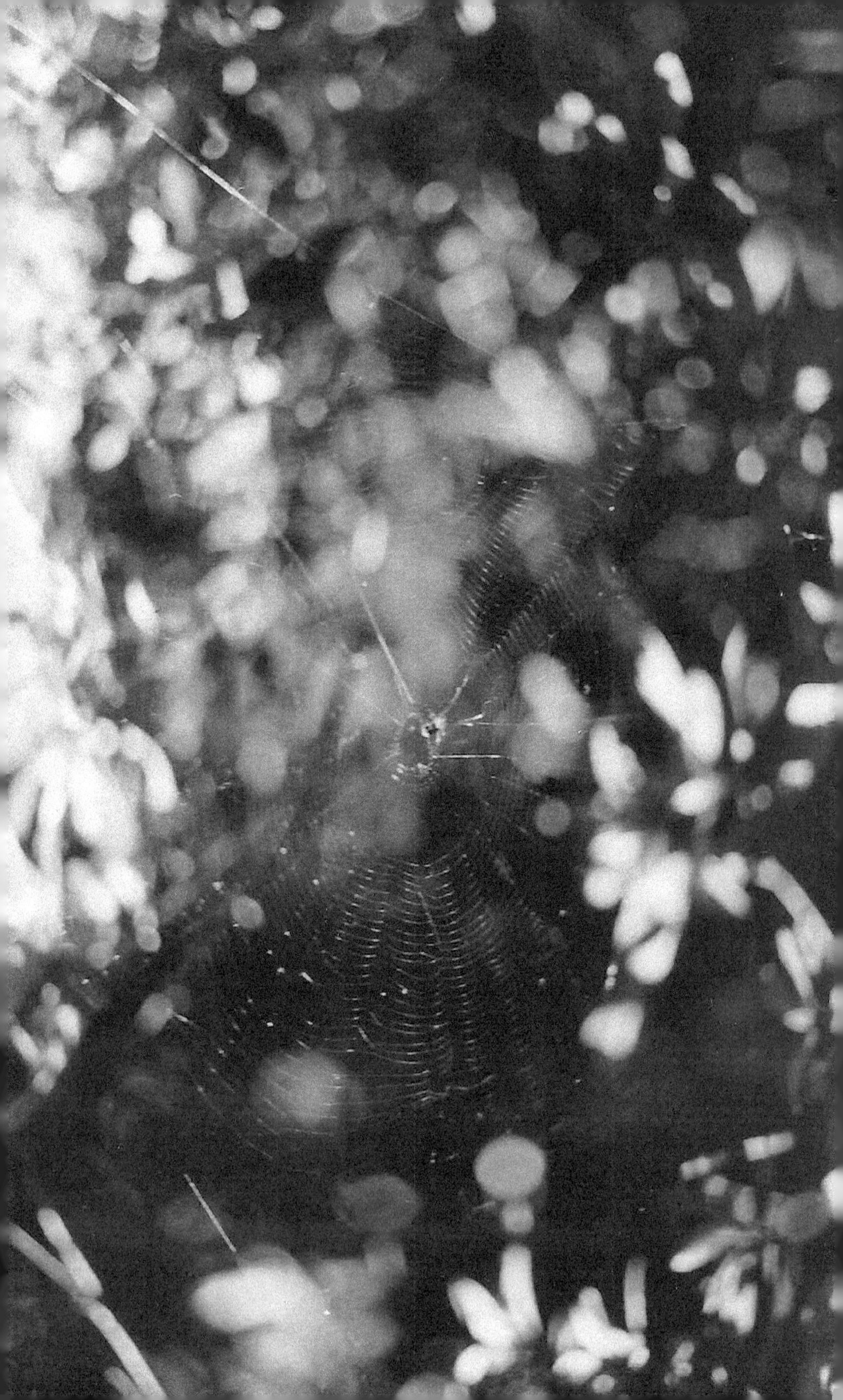

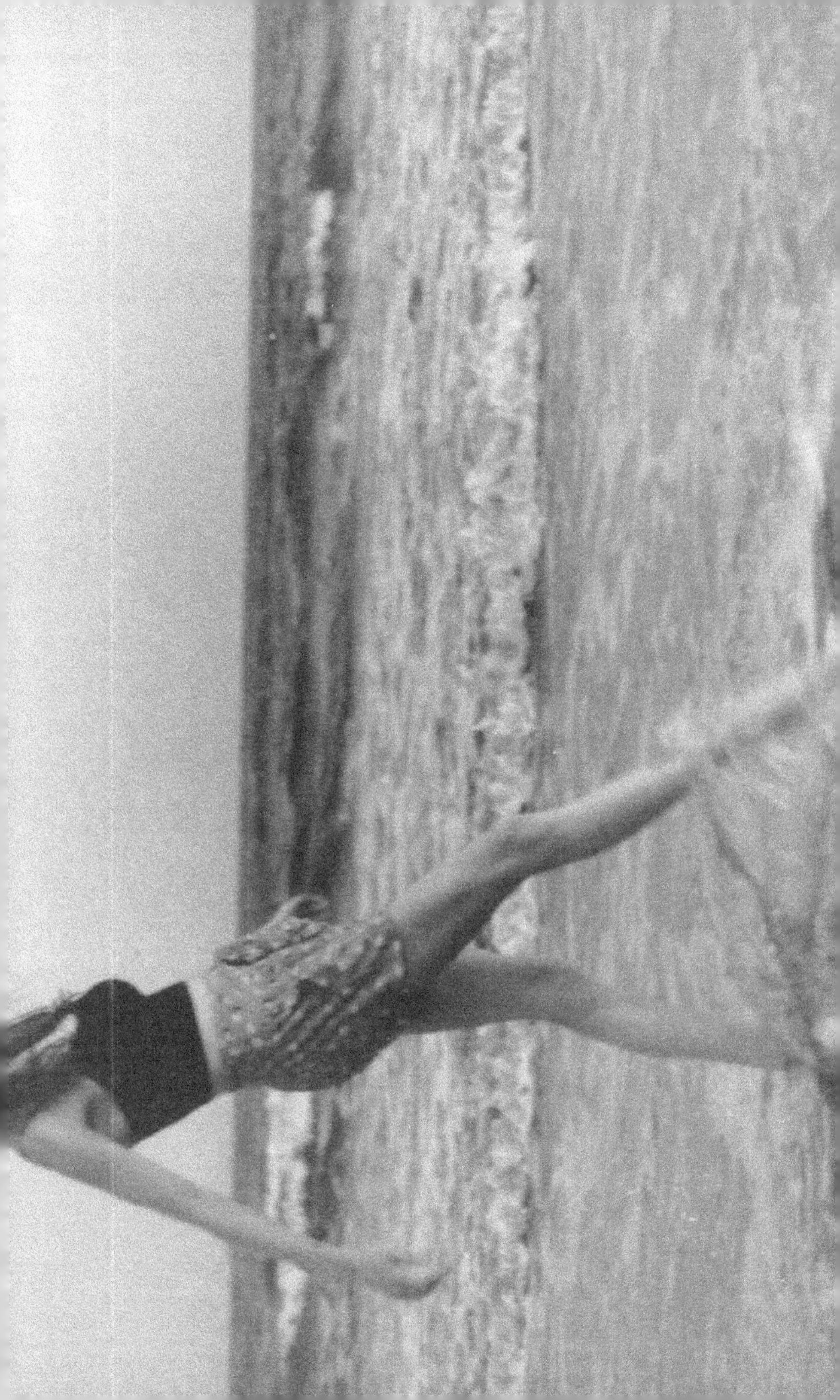

VII

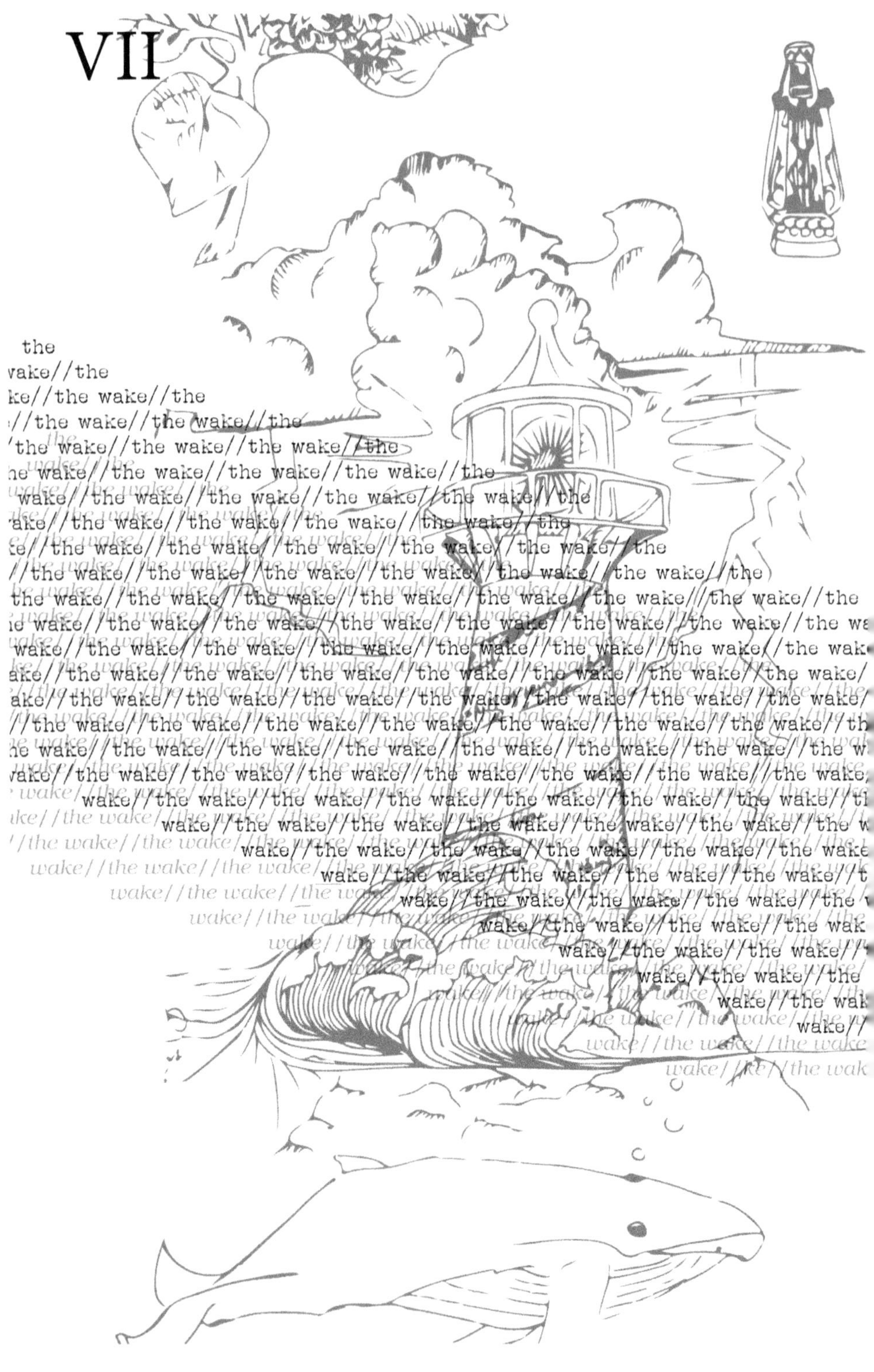

After all, I think you were nothing more than rorschach — mental gymnastics.
Self-reflection, self-flagellation, manifestation of regret, coping with what happened
when I didn't choose you. Who knows what could've been?

There's so much we'll never know, and man creates a god out of every mystery.

I KNOW NOW —
I mistook you for the god that lives inside my own skin.

Before, I saw my future in the blot but now all I see is myself, adorned with blossoms
and laurel,

a bud emerging from every wound.

5/9/23
11:49 pm

al-hallaj

and for the sake of you
i give up the ghost

i give up this sacred
love
we could've been divine
together

but i slide down the pale
instead

i cannot reach you here
i cannot mislead you
in your notions
of your own capacity for love

you need to believe
in the orthodoxy
of the mundane

and at the bottom of the stake
i am tasting god

4/19/23
3:27 pm

everything changes but this
even me
and you
but this-
somehow
i feel the same as always

but i'm not the same

7/31/23
11:31 pm

molting

the air ate half my cigarette
while i realized
i almost didn't make it this far
last summer

photos of bruises
and stretch marks
and grey-yellow scleras
late july

something so beautiful
about the passing of time

kissing girls and collecting shells
alone with the dead bird
on topsail beach

i almost became her
she almost became me
in the way all dead things
are essentially one in the same

the little girl
in my grandmother's frame
she deserved more
than she got

until i learned
how to give it to her.

6/18/23
5:24 pm

albatross necklace
dawn fades into noon
our love is reckless,
wolves yearning for the moon

they walked from me
so i could come to you.

4/23/23
9:20 pm

i woke up out of myself

4/26/23
8:32am

i think
we're meant to be in love
just
not with each other.

you sure taught me a lesson, alright.
yeah, you sure taught me.

12/10/22
4:27 pm

(perhaps you will be the rain)

the truth is that one day
all things must turn to something new
we churn in the consumer

the truth is that one day
my body will feed flowers in the dew
but something will last longer

my flowers will want you
as i do
as i do

1/26/23
12:41 pm

if you think i didn't notice you walking out

— i did

but i was scared you'd run if i followed

that maybe if i told you
one more time
that you mean something to me

you'd vanish

i'd rather you be far away
than watch your place in my mind dissolve
into the nothing

this meaning,
something can be both so precious
and so far away

besides,

all i want is for you to be happy
that doesn't have to include me,
not if you don't want

5/4/23
10:45 am

how the monolith
fell so quietly
i do not know

you'd think
it would've been a violent death

but i have not thought of you
i have not thought of you

ambivalence in my bones
it's up to you now.

5/5/23
12:14 am

you're bubbling up tonight.
in my heart
maybe i'll never let you go
maybe it won't be every couple of days.
maybe it'll be weeks
or months
or years
when you'll cross my mind.

i tried everything to get rid of you
but i think you'll always be here
and i know i'll always remember you.
or maybe i'll just —
remember the hope.

the way i wanted you.
all i know is that
i'll remember something.
the way i loved.
and
the way i love.
always.

don't think you vanished.
i let you disappear
in the way you always wanted to.

5/5/23
12:36 am

clinging to an idea
like a life raft

but you sank
and i drowned with us

heartbreak
i sucked the marrow
and i inhaled the smoke

hookah in the evening
a pathfinder
and a follower

i just wanted you
but you'd never trust that.

maybe you'll pick this up
and understand

i hope you're happy out there.
i do.
(something i gave up on saying)

3/20/23
1:21 pm (abridged)

he asked
do you touch yourself when you think of me?
but he touched me
while he thought of himself

nothing here was worth holding on to

and so we both walked
in different directions
clutching pieces of ourselves
bypassing the way we
were supposed to hold on
because precious things can be too heavy
for the miles we must go
on tired feet

6/14/23
12:15 pm

i may not always be what you need
sometimes, ill be the opposite of that
rarely, we'll see eye to eye

but one thing is true—
i'll never leave your side.

friends.

i'll always be your friend.

5/24/23
12:42 pm

funny that i wrote all these beautiful words for a liar

i am afraid to open

if i read it

my chest will split
like the red sea

fish on either side
trapped in frozen waves
watching me step into the crack
and walk my way back
collecting shells along the way
scraps of memory
precious
words
in the silence
we held in our mouths
lips open
secrets sealed between us
in a kiss

if i open
i might go too wide
and shatter
a crystal glass
filled with baby carriages
and good cuts of meat
and a walk through the market
where we said a lot
but spoke little
the first thing
to touch me
after the demolition
broke every bone
dropped

i'm brining
in my own blood
and his

reckless hopes
that fate may have me follow
date to date
back to him

i want to open
right now
urgently

i want to open and
touch in pixels
something so fine
and gentle
the german shepherd puppy face
eyes so big
round marble mirrors
rolling around lighting up the road
ahead of
jarred innocence
a glass skull
clear, in honesty
so clean i can see
everything happening inside
in perfect clarity

and i know it is so good
too good for a woman
who fucked the very next day
post-departure
mystery tears misting
another man's chest
he didn't understand
because i wouldn't tell him

too good for a woman
with a crawl space heart
where everyone and all the trash gets shoved

but he would disagree with me here
wouldn't mind
the way i chose to deal
the cards unfairly
in a state of shock

and, i will repeat myself
because it needs to be clear—
i want to open
throw myself
through the time and space
my heart is unfamiliar with
but it hurts bad

and so i wait

maybe this afternoon, i think
i'll open
in a bit

or maybe
i'll turn a deadbolt

spare us both
from having to
drag a flashlight
under the house
and dig up all the bones
we left behind

2/7/23
7:34 pm

vlad

you are the spike
i perpetually impale myself upon
the whip
the cilice
around my thigh
the rough cloth on my skin
that i choose to wrap
around myself

you were right
when you said
it's not your fault
i made your holes in me
i shot myself
i devoted myself
to the idea of you
thought maybe you'd be my afterlife

assumed there would be
a reward
for prayer
but i was wrong

you were an error
but not a mistake
my prize is growth

2/1/23
2:42 am

dissonance

it's the itch
between two puzzle pieces
left on the table—

disconnected

i've never seen something so perfect
lay incomplete
ambivalent
like the empty side of the bed

the ache in my chest informs me
this won't be an easy recovery

2/7/23
8:04 pm

1

everyone is concerned
with body counts
and bases

but they shouldn't be
because i've got something
much worse

i have skeletons in my heart
i take them out at night
and sharpen the bones

i cut myself to bleed
onto a page

i have scars on my face
the other boys really don't like—
most are from you

i have something vile
graphic
favorite beheadings
hollow words never spoken
bones in a black bag

endings i chose

in spite of pain
and this is so much worse
than a fuck
this is a hand full of forever
sprinkled like pixie dust, glitter
this is *i thought about you while i baked a pumpkin pie*
and on a ride to the funeral home,
i thought of you while i held my grandma's hand
i cried to my father about you
and i still lost
and i still love
even though it's gone

this is much worse
than a body between my sheets
that will be gone in the morning
because you never even
laid down next to me
and i made a monster of you

a shadow in my closet
that scares me awake
but i learned, also,
to live without you
it was the only way
to keep you with me
and i really don't see
why my body count matters
i'd hate to be a number
other than 1
like you
but there will be more

and one day
someone will love my multitudes

they will love you
with me
because you're inside me
and then they will mean more than you

someone will consume us both

he will do the work required
to become bigger than you
a rosetta stone

reading the words between us
i can't understand
making sense of what
i was trying to fill with you
whatever gap you exploited
and when he kisses the scars
they'll fade
and you'll fade
to number **2**

5/17/23
1:36 pm

i associate you with a small collection of places
in which i hoped
for us

7/6/23
10:01 pm

exit wound

i grieved everything that happened on the path i did not take;
i grieved everything that happened on the path i did
and now
i am new

2/6/23
8:32 am

DEAD BIRD II

i am lacing my boots
and you should be worried
i am picking up my keys
and you should be worried
i am opening the door and stepping out
and you should be worried
and i would stay if you asked
and come back to bed
i am closing the door
and you should be worried
i am driving away
and you should be worried
i am taillights in the distance
and you should be worried
and i would turn around if you asked
but you didn't ask
you didn't even notice i packed a bag

i wish you had looked up
maybe one day you will
and you'll wonder where i went

while you stood at the window
guessing at the color of the sky
i am flying a mile high
my eyes still on your back

7/17/23
11:09pm

my eyes.
on the horizon.

the air.

lilith

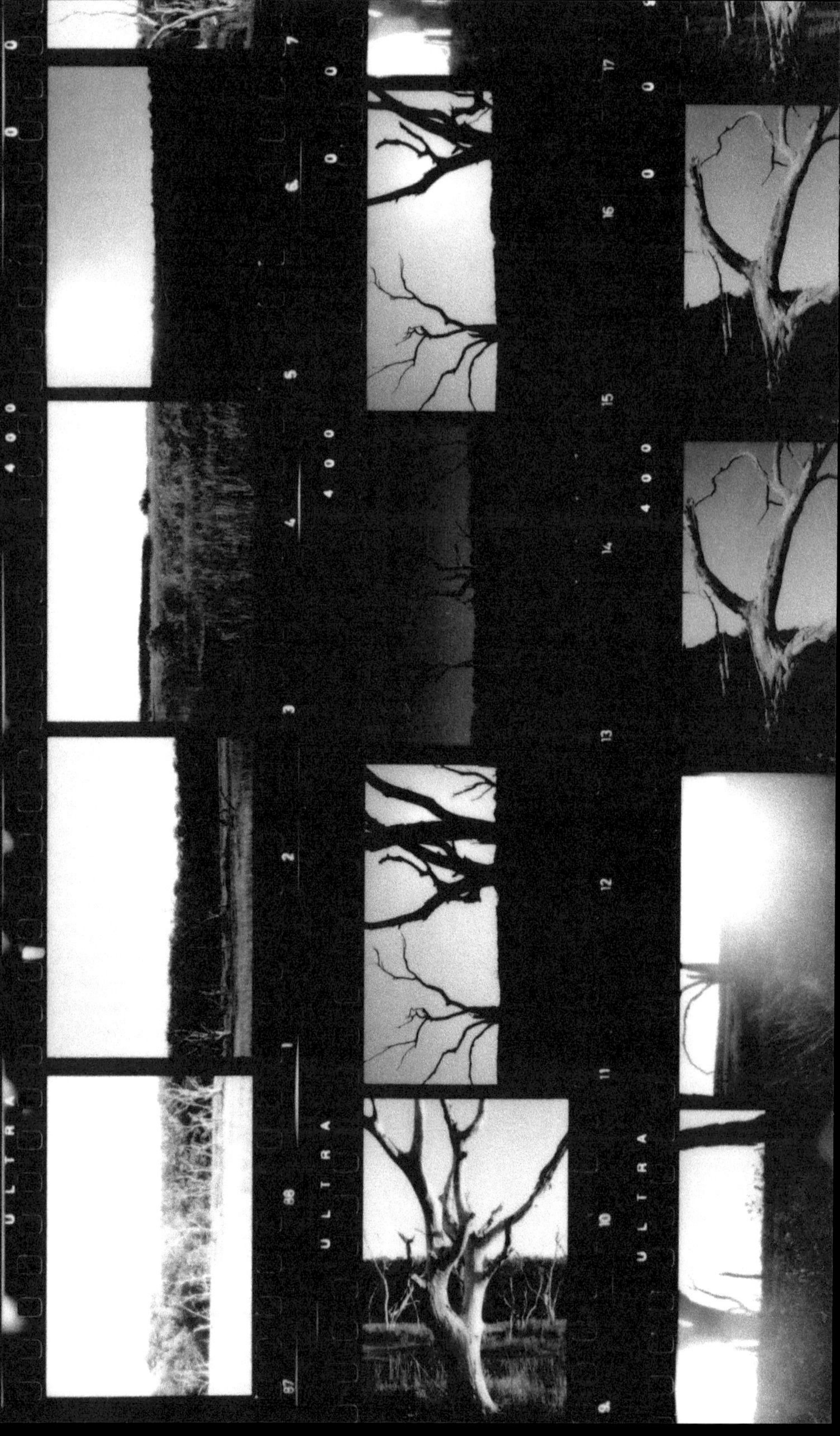

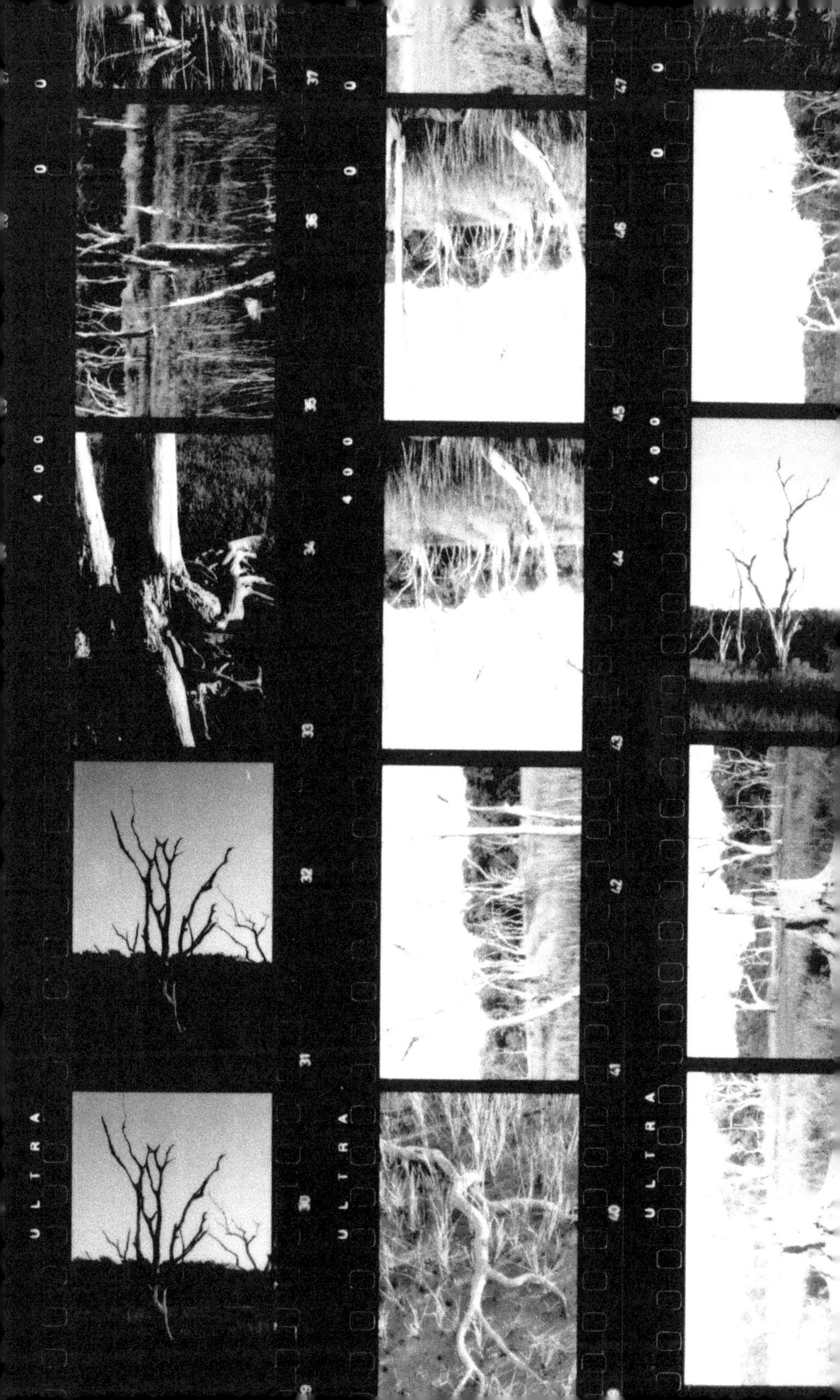

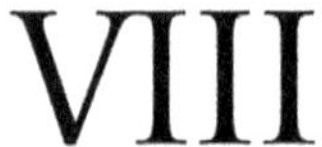

kintsugi//kintsugi//kintsugi//kintsugi//kintsugi

kintsugi//kintsugi//kintsugi//kintsugi//kintsugi kintsugi//kintsugi//kintsugi//kintsugi//kintsugi

kintsugi//kintsugi//kintsugi//kintsugi//kintsugi kintsugi//kintsugi//kintsugi//kintsugi//kintsugi

//kintsugi//kintsugi//kintsugi//kintsugi kintsugi//kintsugi//kintsugi//kintsugi

//kintsugi//kintsugi//kintsugi//kintsugi//kintsugi//kintsugi//kintsugi//kintsugi//kintsugi

even
the pain
was
perfect

wednesday
7/19/23
12:39am

hopscotch

1

there

is a boy
in your bedroom and you are alone
in the house

everybody left
for the weekend
so you commence with

the only thing left to do

an awkward shuffle
a pinch of pain

you don't
really want this.

you don't know what you want

you'll think of another while
he looks shocked and lucky
and fills you with birdshot
and the feeling of wind in your ear turning into
an ache
acidic
between your tongue and the roof
of your mouth.

the things that come after the things that can't be taken back.

you don't know it now
but he will hurt you and
hurt you
and hurt you

for crimes like
not being fun
and being smarter than him
and for not being like the girls
in the videos.

you will learn to be like them
sooner or later

you will learn
to be less

(of yourself)

and more like
an all you can eat
buffet

although the word
rattles around your mouth
a pinball that never hits the pop bumpers

you'll learn to call it a pussy.

2

there is a new
boy

the walls are red
and blue
there is weed stomped into the carpet

maybe
this one won't hurt
like that

you're right— saccharine sweet
this one will
almost kill you.

he will teach you to hate
the space between skin
and muscle

the honeycomb matrix of feather-down pillows
and sponge cake
just above the uterus
and the flesh that provides compression
between your

thighs.

he will
try to watch you die.

you will have to be physically
removed from him
booked into a facility
that will drain the poison from your veins.

you will not
laugh
for a while
without it sounding like ipecac meeting stomach acid

you will recoil

from every touch
but not like a kicked dog— you're a gun now.

you will add locks to your doors. so many locks. swearing,

no-one will ever
hurt you and
hurt you
and hurt you ever again.

your friends will call you the strongest person they know. but you're not, you're just

numb.

3 *(almost forgot about this one.)*

you're sitting in a recruitment bonus shaped like a dodge charger.
you will notice it is a six-cylinder (lame)
but he bought you dinner
and he accidentally said "i love you" when he closed the door behind you
which raised more questions than you were willing to unpack
so you laughed about it
this made you more willing to forget   *that he lied about his height.*

he will ask if you want to drive to the   *beach*
which— you both know what that means
you're about to fuck in a parking lot for no reason
which at this point, will feel like reason enough.

the first foreign object to   *make landfall in 8 years*
doesn't feel good but doesn't feel bad either
you will wonder if maybe this is your fault

he shows you pictures of his family in   *utah*
he tells you in detail how you might get along with each of them

(the kids would love you)
he follows you home on a road with no street lights
texting you "do you own any langeray" (the typo kind of disgusts you, but you swallow it back)
the last you see of him is   *lacing boots.*

4

this one will lay in your
bed

and tell you about the problems
in the lives of the three or four other girls
he is dating

but he's staying the whole weekend
and you can't forget that you are so so cool. not
like them. (you are just like them.)

you will sleep next to him in ripped
fishnets (the ones he requested)

hoping
to be selected.

you will overlook.
he has lost count of how many people he has been with
you are just a fish; nothing more

he will come back to your door every time he fails another

he will cry to you about them after he
takes your last bastion
you will let him
you will not hesitate.

he hits you you asked him to.
you like it that way, these days.

5

this one will show up out of nowhere
a friend of a friend with a south african accent, materializing behind you
on a sun-scorched beach day
in early may.

running into the surf, you will look your friend dead in the eye and declare your intentions for him
she will laugh, in an appalled sort of way,

she knows you're capable of it

in two days, you'll meet again, this time at your house
he will check his reflection in the glass of your front door before knocking,

he will be sweet
he will know every record in your collection

he will stay   late

until your friends leave
and, as you slow dance in the kitchen
he will kiss you softly

which will turn to savagery in a matter of moments

you will not know this is the first time he's ever done this kind of thing before

certainly, you're no veteran

he will kiss his way down your belly, gripping you tightly in a gentle sort of way
you will think
"wow this could be a kind of happy i could hold forever"

and by the time it's all over
he will try to tuck you into bed

"no, i'm not going to sleep yet, i need to do the dishes,"

"well, goodnight. i had a wonderful time"

"don't let this be the last time i see you"

"it definitely won't be, i promise"

you'll be half-certain you will never see him again.

you'll be right.

you'll take no lessons from this.

6

you used to
be afraid
of the disease inside the men
that reduced you to chicken breast
and bandages

but they did you the kindness
of infection.

this one will sit across from you
over french fries
listen to all of the above

he will tell you
his brother died
two years ago.

you will feel minimally about this.

you will watch the idea
make landfall in his mind—

you.
you could be the one. maybe

you will laugh inside
the error noise a computer makes when you hit the wrong command key.

you will take him home anyways
you will feel a little bad about this
because you know this means more to him
rule number 1 is have fun!—

he lets you know
you are the first woman to ever sit in his car (he bought it four months ago)
waking up on his chest will fill your bloodstream with panic

why

is he still here?

you will block him after communicating that you do not want to see him again. in approximately 1 month, he will make a fake online profile, posing as a woman. you will accept, assuming he is a friend you made at the bar. in 2 months, from this profile, he will send you a photo, unprompted. in this photo, he will be holding his erect penis as though he is brandishing a sword. the caption will be "i love you <3"

you will cry about this. you will feel that everything you presumed to be genuine from him is false. the fact that you never want to see him again will not have any impact on this. you will feel that you cannot be trusted with yourself.

7

he will show up to your house in those shoes that click into bike pedals.
you will sit and just talk for a few hours
you will discover that he is younger than you. not too young for this, no.

but you feel a pang
of guilt

an errant thorn catching you
as you reach for a blackberry.

when he kisses you, he is bad at it

he will inquire about this
and you will tell him he is good.

he will whisper
oh
my
god.
ican'tbelievethisishappening

and just like that, you will call the whole thing off
milk chocolate is too sweet for you

you will acknowledge to yourself that he is just a wrench
for grief
an oxytocin fix
but one you are unwilling to swallow guilt over

you will ask to be friends
he will agree and smile
like this is just as good an option to him
you will be glad you did this

you will drive him home, his bike clanging around the bed of your pickup,
when you get home yourself, you will lock the deadbolt and put your back to the door so you can breathe better
a monster self-aware enough to lock its own cage.

8

you thought you were all friends. you were supposed to be friends but now

you cannot move
eyes open, body involuntarily limp
they will underestimate your weight just enough to
make this spectacular
fireworks of pain a cloud thought drifts across the sky you
are visualizing in your Happy Place

i am definitely going to piss blood

something tasted funny earlier and now you are strung up like a wild
boar about to be skinned

you will wake up with bruises and
your mouth will taste like you slept with 4¢ under your tongue

theyhurtyouandhurtyouandhurtyouandhurtyou.

you don't speak the same language
but you figure "no" is pretty universal
you said it before the substance entered your bloodstream through the side door, though
maybe that changed things.

everything is on fire
crawling into the shower
you will not know that the screaming you hear
is coming from your own open mouth
until later when you stop because you are choking, silently.

you ran

out of sound.
things are quiet now, in the way that it is quiet

inside of a casket.

you will crawl out of the shower
and feel like you failed.
because somebody hurt you and hurt you and hurt you again.

you will lay on the floor
and stare at the popcorn ceiling

you will not be able to feel the breath
in your chest
unless it is accompanied by *burning tobacco*
for at least a week.

you will not let them take this from you
you will swear to prove that they haven't.

this is a death, of sorts.
you will be aware of the things that happened before and after this, perhaps forever.

9

this boy took you to the farmer's market a month ago
then left town for three weeks.

he feels safe
moving slowly
kissing

softly
it's like steamed broccoli
in the sense that you don't really like it
but you're doing it because you know it's probably good for you.

you don't know what love is
so you will hope that maybe this is it?
(you will know that you are wrong, even as you hope)

he will say
lay back
get comfy
hey, look me in the eyes
things like this.

you can't feel it in your body. you will act like you do. your chest will be hopeful. you are not
being hit, at
least.

he will hurt you too.
you don't understand yet but he leaves tomorrow for fucking australia

you will cry and curse the u.s. government
he will tell you he found out on short notice
that he is heartbroken about leaving you
that he hopes you'll wait

you'll be informed later (by someone other than him) that he lied the whole time.

you will spit don't call me baby if you don't mean it

but all of this will happen only after you
pluck
the black tiffany ring
from your left little finger
and make him promise to return it one day

you will decide you hope you never see that ring again,

not even in the mailbox.

10

this one is a negotiator
you will have no objection
no reason is enough reason
at this point

it is monday
and the other man left for san diego 8 hours ago

your ring blissfully unaware that it will never see you again
riding along with him on a chain, resting against his chest

you will not remember how any of this felt
even a moment after it occurred
you do not care

he spits in your mouth. this is good.

you will think— i feel dirty because i am.

but at least i can still do this.

you sit between innings and he will talk about how he thinks his friends
are mostly very stupid.

and you will realize you don't really like him.
he doesn't like you either— you can tell.
you will be acutely aware that he is probably going to text you in exactly one week
to ask for a re-run of all of this. you will decide that you will not respond. you will be correct.

however
nothing feels safe right now
so you hope that he will stay the night
he won't.

tattoos crawl across his whole body
you trace them while he
talks about money. tigers and
dragons
and skeletons with scythes

when he leaves you will be glad he is gone
you didn't feel a thing

but you knew you were touching him *you could see it happen*
you will become aware that none of the sensory information from this experience will be saved on the hard drive. you will think

perhaps i am broken, forever, finally.

perhaps all you can do from now on *is take an even trade.*

11

this one told you before

that he finds you annoying *but also, beautiful.*
he will text you, three weeks after asking for space

to apologize for his words
he will show up to your house on a tuesday night
high on oxycontin
you will *kiss his neck*
and in the middle of all of this

he will tell you he was abused *as a little boy*
by several different female relatives.

he will say, hold me tighter

but you will recoil, abruptly, at this information
this time *not like a gun.*

he will say
please
don't
stop.

he will look as though he is crying. but you will feel his disdain for you, even as he is asking you to save him.

you will try to do what he claims he needs, before deciding this is altogether a bad decision.
you will refuse.
you will ask to be friends instead
and he will find a way to look both hateful and relieved at the same time.
you will understand this, on a personal level. you will feel it in your sternum. you will see it like a mirror.

he will sit *and tell you all of the things that cycle through him*
take you for a ride on every single cart on the ferris wheel

everything that happens to him at 3am

and then he will stand up *and abruptly leave*

shame and pride blending on his face *into a dark grey*

you will wonder if you will ever see him again. you will wonder if he will be an obituary you find on Google.

12 (two feet on the ground.)

as he steps out your front door, going home for more oxycontin,
you will
once again press your back against it and slide to the floor.

the monster will slide the chain into place and cry herself to sleep.

you know nothing about being kissed first
you cannot feel your own lips
or fingertips
or the air pushing out of the vent weaving its way through your hair and into your lungs

you do not know this yet
but this is almost the last page.

tomorrow
you will go to waffle house . you will not expect it.

it will be wednesday
nobody told you the bible was wrong
nobody told you the world

started
on a wednesday in may

you will
laugh. you will feel air between your ribs

and he will

kiss you first.

...

on a day in late june, you will say to him what you said to the others.

"i

want you

to fuck me like you hate me"

he will refuse.
he will be the first to do that.

.

you will decide that maybe you know what love is.

13

one day you will wake up different
on a morning a week after *shedding your own blood*
for the first time in seven years

you will not want anything

except yourself

you'll be tired *of all this*

the self-destruction
demolition for the sake of love

you always said that women tend to be speed bumps or lessons to men, until they are ready to love for real. but now you'll realize— this applies to you too. there is no gender distinction to a wound.

the discounts you gave
drinking to drown it
the begging
the hoping
floundering in the shallows

you will remember
who you are
and everything before this moment
will seem absurd

a good story, sure
but just a story now

baptized in the lines of sunlight
slipping between your blinds

it'll be simple
and easy
and also, kind of sad
discarding all the things you believed you needed
looked forward to having
in exchange for the choice to be happy right now

it'll come out of nowhere
a bubble popping
a supernova
a sprout worming its way through the soil

finally lifting its face to the sun

budding contentment
you'll suddenly want for nothing
you'll choose
you

and although you'll have a lot, really, that'll always be more than enough.

6/5/23
4:22 pm

Could i give this all up——
every foreign territory
i could claim by touch
every other field
upon which
i could bound for an hour

to begin
laying bricks?

there is safety in transience
having no home,
adapting to cloud-form
means nobody can rob you

(you have nothing to take)

with a single fond memory
it's easy to let go
without looking down;
you didn't climb very high

but tasting everything
going one spoonful at a time
has put a dent in my chest
and slit my tongue
down the middle.

because i move fast
burning curiosity
shoveling fears into the engine

stopping for a moment
just to speed off at
90, breathless irish goodbyes
telling myself——

none of these places
cared to have me anyways.

they all look different
but everything feels the same
when you're numb
perpetually shaking off
pins and needles
still in shock
from taking the last good beating
on the chin.

a few weeks ago
i got off
and felt the light on my skin
for a moment
gold and black—the new moon
called me out
away from the tracks

my unspoken questions
heavy in the air

will you hurt me?
will you love me?

floating bubbles
hanging stars

then i woke up
rain-soaked
flat on my back

thinking
i've never seen a cloud fall, before

but how the hell do i get back up?

now naked,
no getaway car
or buoyancy
shot down like a bird-
praying not to see an albatross
in the mirror

heart too heavy to catch the wind
full
of something that feels
resplendent and like
swallowing tacks
in equal turns

toeing the edge of my own territory
border crossing negotiations
with thistles between my toes

surveying the crack
realizing
we could build a home
here.

babe, check the radar— is it supposed to rain today?

(will i float away?)

or

are you thinking
what i'm thinking?

Afterword

These poems are written to an archetype, pieced together from all my good memories of men who supported and loved me once. These words illustrate my journey of loving (and then transcending) a part of me that craved dependence upon someone outside of myself—a person who does not exist and ultimately could not help me even if they did.

The subject(s) of these poems may be people, but really, every stanza was a conversation with myself. The ego is captured in battle with my values and higher knowing. Through observing myself experiencing a limerent state for a number of months following a major trauma, I became acutely aware of myself and the tendencies I had that perpetuated my pain.

I also learned much about my own worth. Through reflecting on the moments in which I felt both completely insane and justifiably tangled up in a fantasy, I was able to distill my desires and dissect them at the root.

The pain of my limerence was not because the love I felt was impossible, it was the result of trauma-based patterns I learned in childhood and a deep need for healing and integration of my unconscious desires.

The subjects of desire that limerent people focus on tend to embody qualities that they feel they lack in themselves. There is a "glimmer," or a moment when everything clicks, and you can see yourself with this person, except because you are with them, you are better and more fulfilled than you ever believed you could be.

That glimmer is a spark that can be taken either as a sign that this person is your soulmate, or as a moment of inspiration, a vision that this person has generously bestowed upon you, of the version of yourself that you so deeply desire to step into with or without that person in your life. I learned about the version of myself I had repressed, that I had been yearning to become. I got stronger, more balanced, more assertive of my needs, and more willing to take risks. I learned how to give myself the comfort I was craving.

Through this, I realized that my experience with limerence was reflective of the disempowerment I experienced in times when I depended upon a man to fulfill me, and oftentimes minimized myself in order to be more palatable, to be chosen.

Just like that, the limerence withered.

I learned to not sprint ahead, to build love brick-by-brick, and to respond not to dreams and fantasies, but to actions and displays of morality and character.

I released myself from the shackles of the concept of The ONE, and discovered a version of myself that exists happily outside of attachment or high-stakes love games.

Regarding the concept of The One, there are hundreds, if not thousands of people on this planet that can and will love you. There's a handful of people you could be absolutely happy spending your life with. If it's not working out, the person you're betting on is probably not one of them. Don't worry, you've got more than one shot at this, so long as you are brave. You are worthy of the love you desire, and the love meant for you is a love in which you are accepted exactly as you are.

No one person is the answer, especially when the love you desire is locked away inside of you.

The person you desire handed you a key that opens a part of you that has the potential to be actualized. Thank them for the key, but don't mistake them to be the doorway through which you must go in order to become fulfilled.

For anyone who has or currently is experiencing limerence, I recommend
Love and Limerence: The Experience of Being in Love, by Dorothy Tennov.

I also recommend assessing your attachment style, journaling, and reality-testing.

Oftentimes, we are limerent about someone inaccessible to us because we are emotionally unavailable and scared of the vulnerability and risk that comes with falling in love.

I promise you, you will never find a zero-risk love. To love is to lose, one way or another. There is no way around it. Get to know yourself, learn to care for yourself, and be your own home. You will find you are capable of more than you ever thought. You will discover yourself as someone who can withstand the risk and loss associated with love, and that you are deserving of being loved by someone who can do the same. All the love you felt for this person is a reflection of the boundless nature of your heart, of your own ability to love uninhibited.

My recommendation is to learn to turn that love towards yourself. If you can love yourself as much as you loved that person you spent hours, days, months, yearning for, you'll find yourself capable of more than you ever knew.

For everyone who took the journey through these pages with me, thank you. I created this collection because I wanted to share a journey through my own heart. To everyone who understood— I love you. We are the proud owners of brave hearts and wistful minds.

- Lilith.

Acknowledgements

To my family, especially ***my father and mother****, who, in spite of me being the Prodigal Daughter, have supported my dreams unconditionally. To* ***Marcus Amaker****, who has been my mentor, a source of inspiration, and most importantly, my friend. Your encouragement means the world.*

To ***Ava, Jordyn, Jenna, Mel, Erin, Jackie, Lexie****, and* ***all the women in my life*** *who have kept my feet planted firmly in moments when I have been determined to live with my head in the clouds, and who have picked me up in moments that razed me to the ground. My real love story is you girls.*

To ***Katherine****, for your incredible friendship, wisdom, and kindness.*

To ***Hinnah and Sresh****, for being the shining example I needed of what real love looks like (especially for a poet).*

To ***Corey,*** *Vishnu thanks Vishnu for the guidance.*

And finally, to ***Sam Richardson****, without whom, this project never would have been completed. You have kept me sane, been my reality check, talked me through a million-and-one C-PTSD episodes, and have never once made me feel crazy for literally being insane. You have also helped compile every poem in this book, collaborated with me on every design, stenographered many an unhinged 'OOF.exe' journal entry, listened to every dramatic voice memo, and procured sushi for me in times of great need. We're gonna build that cabin. SameBrain, SameBladder.*

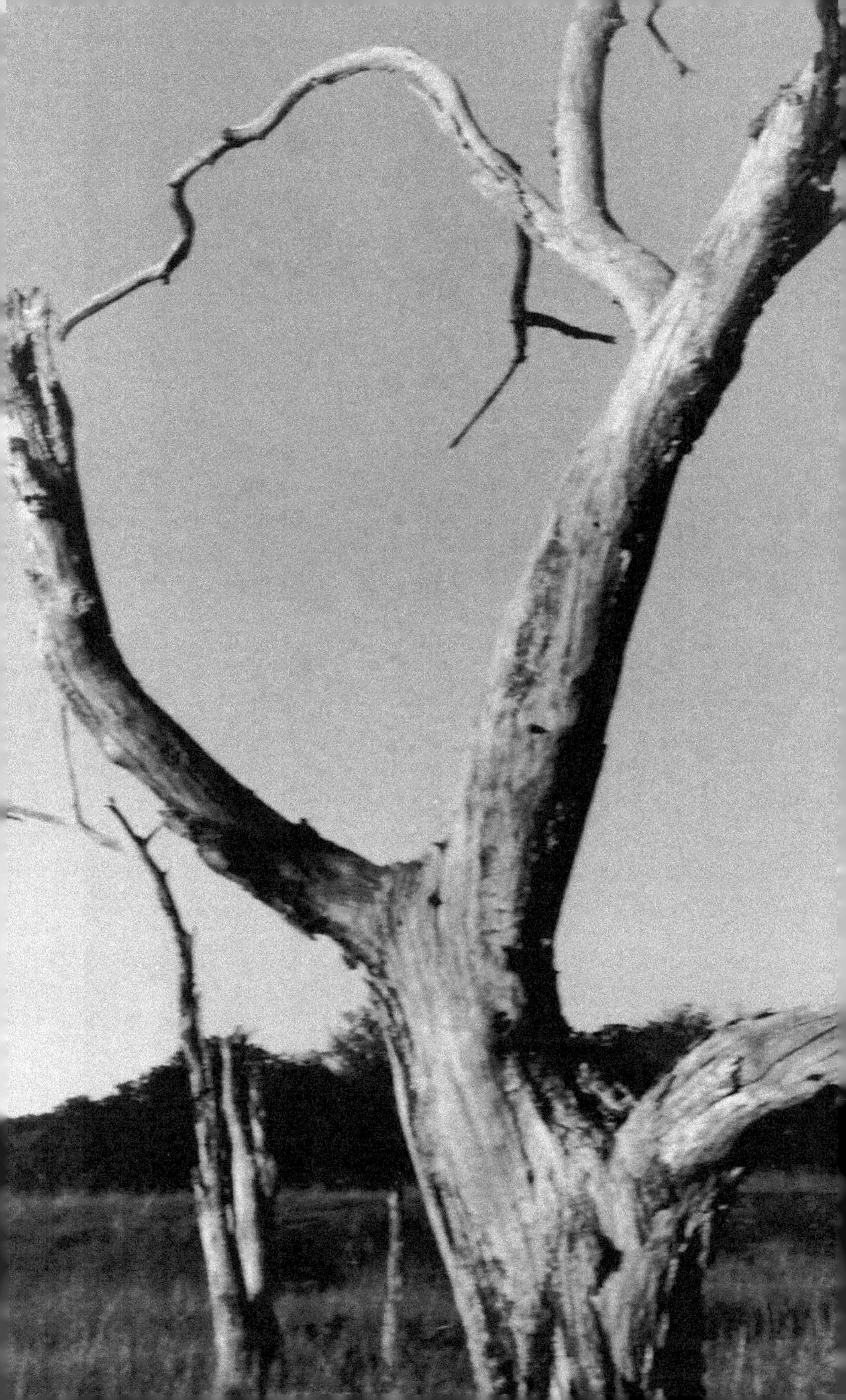

the light crawls across wet pavement. . .